Women in Flight Research at NASA Dryden Flight Research Center from 1946 to 1995

I0155797

by
Sheryll Goecke Powers

NASA History Office
Code ZH
NASA Headquarters
Washington, DC 20546

Monographs in
Aerospace History
Number 6
1997

Table of Contents

Cover photo: NASA Photo E212, group photograph of women by snowman, late 1948.

Design and layout: Steven Lighthill, Visual Information Specialist, Dryden Flight Research Center.

Preface

My initial plan for this study was to discuss the women with engineering degrees who worked at Dryden throughout its history. However, until the 1970s not many women with engineering degrees worked at Dryden. In addition, until the late 1960s, many of the women (and men) who worked in the engineering, or technical, field at Dryden had degrees in the sciences (math, physics, etc.) instead of engineering. Another reason I changed my topic was because during the early years at Dryden, the women with non-engineering degrees (in some cases, no degree) performed the same work as a junior engineer. Also, during my years at Dryden, I heard many stories about the early days concerning the people, the work and the living conditions. Despite the initial negative feelings for the climate and living conditions, all were enthusiastic about the work and all had fond memories of that time. I decided to focus my discussion on those times and on the contributions of the women in the engineering field for those times.

I began working at the NASA Flight Research Center at the end of May in 1963. Eight of us, two of us women, had come as aerospace engineering co-ops from Iowa State University in Ames, Iowa. The term "co-ops" refers to the students in a cooperative work-study program between NASA and different universities, technical and vocational schools. Students alternate between work periods at a NASA site and course work at the school. The length of the work periods depends on the school. My schedule was to work three 6-month periods and one 3-month period (the last work period). Being in the co-op program caused my graduation date to slip a year. However, the co-op program has the definite benefits of gaining work experience and earning money. I am one of many co-ops hired at Dryden over the years. During my years at Dryden, I worked on projects involving the Lunar Landing Research Vehicle, X-15, XB-70, YF-12, F-111 Transonic Aircraft Technology research vehicle, F-111 Mission Adaptive Wing, space shuttle and X-29.

The by-hand techniques used for data reduction and analysis when I began working in 1963 were extremely labor intensive. In fact, these techniques were the same as used by the first contingent to arrive at Dryden in September 1946. This labor-intensive effort affected all aspects of engineering including the effort to produce camera-ready copies for the NACA and NASA series reports. The data reduction techniques are discussed in the text. I will mention the reporting procedure here. Some of the early NACA reports (very few of the NASA reports) used the hand-drawn plots of the author for the camera-ready versions. Usually, the data plots the author made were in turn traced in ink by a technical illustrator (always men until the late 1970s or early 1980s). The technical illustrator also used his considerable talent to improve (or provide) sketches or drawings for the reports. The author's handwritten text, which usually had arrows or other notations to indicate inserts that were to be included or sentences that were to be moved, was first typed by the branch secretary. The author made minor changes to this typed text on the individual pages. Major changes required cutting, rearranging, and pasting or taping the pages. After the editor (always a woman until the late 1980s) and author agreed on the final version, the camera-ready copy was typed on a manual typewriter by dedicated typists in the report preparation office. Because of the required margins for the camera-ready copies, the text had to fit within a defined area on the page. Adding words could cause the text to exceed the defined area. With luck, the added words were absorbed in a page or two instead of requiring retyping of all pages following the change. Similarly, if too many words were deleted on a page, that page and the pages following would need retyping. Consequently, changes to the final version of the text were made only after much consideration. I remember one of the senior engineers advising me to minimize the words in the figure titles in order to ease the typing burden for the typists. The computer systems of today make changes in the text or data plots very easy.

The changes in the social attitude toward the women engineers, and the other women at Dryden as well, are as dramatic as the changes in engineering task. For example, until the late 1960s to early 1970s, women were expected to wear dresses (or skirts) and shoes with heels and hose. Slacks were permissible only for very rare occasions. This unwritten dress code made it more difficult to do tasks that were easy for the men, such as climbing a ladder to examine the pressure orifices on the top surface of a wing. Today, casual slacks and jeans are as acceptable as more formal dress.

Social attitudes restricted non-work activities as well. One woman, who graduated from college in the late 1950s, told me how concern about reputation had adversely affected her non-work activities. She, her boyfriend and another couple who were also dating wanted to go on a camping trip. But, there was no married couple who could act as chaperones. She decided the trip would be too great a risk to her reputation and did not go. She regretted that decision and wished that she had gone camping. The other woman (not a NASA employee) did go. The woman telling me was considered by all to be very staid and proper. I don't know anyone who could have conceived of her doing anything wild and foolish. By the late 1970s to early 1980s, the attitudes had definitely changed. I remember one story about a young woman of that time who worked at NASA for a few years. The story concerned her and her boyfriend who was a skydiver. On this particular dive, he was attempting to hit a marked ground target. To provide added incentive for him, she stripped and lay in the center of the target. I never heard how close he actually came to the target. I don't even know for sure that the story was true. However, because I knew her, I believe the story. Another change in social attitude concerns women working after marriage. During the early years, most women who married when they were working were expected to quit their jobs soon after, and most did. That isn't true today.

Determining the women who worked at Dryden prior to 1963 was not easy. I used the library card catalog of Dryden authors to find the women authors and co-authors of technical reports. I also used available organizational charts, photographs, old telephone directories, the 1954 Yearbook published by the Air Force of the people who worked at Edwards (with individual photographs by organization), old issues of the Dryden in-house newsletter and the memories of people who worked here during that time. I apologize to any of the women I may have omitted. The additional information resources from 1963 to the present included my memories and the memories of those still working at Dryden.

I would like to thank all the people who shared their memories and experiences with me. In particular, I would like to thank Mary V. Little Kuhl, Mary (Tut) Hedgepeth, Betty Scott Love, Walter C. Williams and Terry J. Larson for their memories of the early days at Dryden and to thank Edwin J. Saltzman and Lannie Dean Webb for sharing their memories and keepsakes from earlier days. Other people who were especially helpful in filling in gaps were Thomas R. Sisk, Johnnye Green Sisk, Gene L. Waltman, Lawrence J. Schilling, Albert E. Kuhl, Wilson E. Vandiver, Cleo M. Maxwell, Paul F. Harney, John W. Smith, Roy G. Bryant, Erma J. Cox, Elizabeth W. Davis, Donald E. Borchers and the Dryden History Committee.

Sheryll Goecke Powers
Dryden Flight Research Center
June 1996

Introduction

Women have been involved with flight research at NASA Dryden Flight Research Center since its inception as the site for flight research on advanced, high-speed aircraft. The first research involved transonic aircraft, including the X-1, the first piloted aircraft to exceed the speed of sound (exceed a Mach number of 1.0). The working environment for the women in the engineering field was influenced by several factors. One factor was the growth of Dryden from 13 or 14 employees (2 of them women) at the end of 1946[1] to the December 1995 size of approximately 450 employees. Other factors include the effect of World War II on the availability of engineers and the advent of digital computers. This monograph describes the working and living environment for the women during the late 1940s and early 1950s. The number of women engineers, their work and the airplanes they worked on from 1960 to December 1995 are also discussed. In order to better understand the labor intensive data gathering and analysis procedures before the age of digital computers, typical instrumentation used on the X-series aircraft from the X-1 through the X-15 is shown. The data reduction technique to obtain the Mach number position error curve for the X-1 aircraft, used to document the historic first flight to exceed the speed of sound, is discussed. A Mach number and altitude plot from an X-15 flight is also shown. The author, employed at Dryden since 1963, used available records along with memory to document the number of women in engineering at Dryden, comment about observed trends, and make personal observations.

Establishment of the NACA Muroc Flight Test Unit

In the early-to-mid 1940s, the National Advisory Committee for Aeronautics (NACA), Army Air Forces, and Navy decided to build and flight test aircraft that could obtain research data in the transonic Mach number region (Mach 0.7 to 1.3). The data were needed to build the next generation of aircraft. This decision was made because the wind tunnels at that time could not reliably obtain the data needed for transonic and supersonic speeds. Also, the interim "short-cut" flight programs of that time, which included air drops of weighted models, launches of models from rockets, and test models mounted on aircraft wings, could not provide all the needed information.

Certain requirements for the flight test area had to be met. One was that the area had to be remote for safety reasons, which included increased landing site availability for the pilot and lessened risk from crashes for the general public. A remote area would also reduce unwanted observation. As is common with most aeronautical advances, there was concern about protecting this research and technology from foreign observers. Another require-

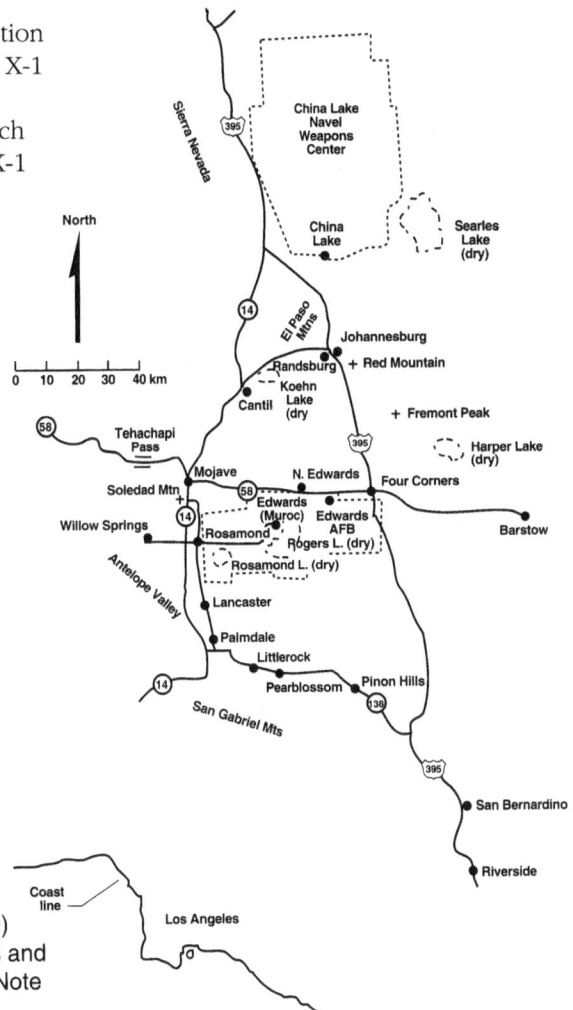

Figure 1. Location of Muroc (Edwards Air Force Base since December of 1949) with respect to Los Angeles. The names and road numbers are for the present time. Note that 40 Km is approximately 25 miles.

1

ment was that the test area have good flying conditions (few cloudy days) because previous NACA Langley flight tests had demonstrated the difficulty in visually tracking aircraft in cloudy skies. The previous flight tests had also shown that these new test aircraft needed long runways for takeoff and landing.

These needs led to the selection of Muroc Army Airfield, which became Muroc Air Force Base in February of 1948 and was renamed Edwards[†] Air Force Base in December of 1949, as the site for the flight tests. Muroc, in the Mojave desert, met the remote location, good flying conditions, and long runways requirements. In addition to the concrete runways, the dry lakebeds at Muroc provided large, natural landing areas. Muroc had two additional advantages. One was that the Army Air Forces, with which the NACA was working, had established Muroc as a wartime center for advanced aircraft testing. The other was the proximity of Muroc to the leading aircraft industries in the Los Angeles area (fig. 1). The employees at the Muroc test site were to conduct flight tests and analyze the data for the rocket-powered XS-1 and the jet-powered and rocket-powered D-558 series of aircraft.[2] The primary purpose of the initial tests was to determine whether the straight-wing XS-1 aircraft and the straight-wing, turbojet-powered D-558 Skystreak aircraft were controllable through the transonic flight regime. The XS-1 aircraft designation, short for Experimental Sonic-1, was renamed the X-1 on 11 June 1948.[3]

The air-launched X-1[††] series aircraft were flight tested from 1946 to 1958 and the D-558 series aircraft from 1947 to 1956. The turbojet engine D-558 Skystreak (D-558-1) aircraft took off under its own power from the ground. Investigations conducted on both

the X-1 and D-558-1 aircraft included the typical flight test studies of wing pressure distributions, lift and drag, stability and control, and handling qualities. Additional testing on the X-1 included the effects of two different wing thickness-to-chord ratios (8% and 10%) and the first use of rocket reaction control jets, which are now used to provide control on all spacecraft including the space shuttle. Additional testing on the D-558-1 Skystreak aircraft included determining the effectiveness of wing vortex generators in improving stability and control and handling qualities. Another version of the D-558 series aircraft (D-558-2) was the 35° leading-edge sweptback-wing Skyrocket aircraft. The Skyrocket was used to test the effectiveness of a sweptback-wing aircraft in the transonic and supersonic flight regimes. One Skyrocket aircraft was powered by both a turbojet engine and a rocket engine and took off under its own power from the ground. An all-rocket engine Skyrocket aircraft was air-launched from a B-29. The third version of the Skyrocket aircraft was also air-launched from a B-29 but had both a turbojet engine and a rocket engine.

In the fall of 1946, NACA Langley began sending people to Muroc. The test

[†] Edwards was named for Captain Glen Edwards (1918-1948), who was killed in the crash of a Northrop YB-49 Flying Wing.

[††] A brief discussion of the flight testing of the X-1 aircraft at Muroc is found in Appendix A, which includes a copy of a special edition of the *X-PRESS*, a publication by and for the employees of the NACA High Speed Flight Station, as Dryden was then designated. The special (or "extra") edition, dated 14 October 1957, was for the 10th anniversary of the first supersonic flight.

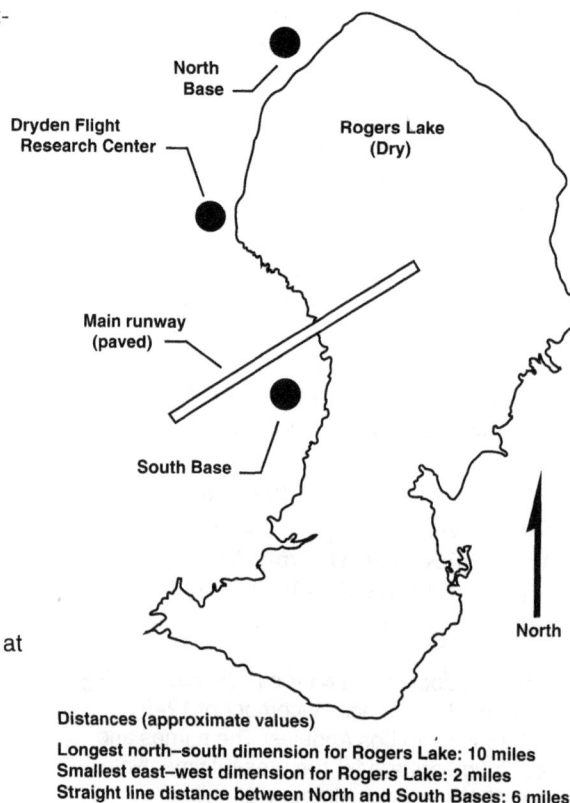

Figure 2. Sketch of Rogers Lake (Dry). Dryden Flight Research Center has been at the location shown since 1954. Presently, the primary flight test area (hangers and support buildings) for Edwards Air Force Base is between the main runway and DFRC.

Distances (approximate values)

Longest north–south dimension for Rogers Lake: 10 miles
Smallest east–west dimension for Rogers Lake: 2 miles
Straight line distance between North and South Bases: 6 miles

facility location was at the South Base† (fig. 2) which was located on the western side of Rogers Dry Lake.†† A contingent of five men arrived on 30 September 1946. Six more men arrived two days before the first glide flight at Muroc of the XS-1 aircraft on 11 October 1946. The first two women, Roxanah B. Yancey and Isabell K. Martin, arrived in December of 1946. The team now consisted primarily of engineers, computers (people who computed), and instrument and telemetry technicians. The computers, following the standard practice of the day, were the two women. In the Federal government's scientific community, almost without exception, the computers were women.

In early September of 1947, NACA decided that the unit at Muroc (now comprised of 27 persons) would function as a permanent facility. The facility, called the·NACA Muroc Flight Test Unit, was managed by NACA Langley. On 14 October 1947, the XS-1 aircraft on its ninth powered flight at Muroc became the first piloted aircraft to fly faster than the speed of sound. This historic flight was followed on 25 November 1947 by the first NACA flight of the D-558-1 aircraft. These flights meant that the people at the NACA Muroc site were now officially involved in the flight testing of both the XS-1 and the D-558 series aircraft.

The history of the establishment of the NACA Muroc site from its beginning in 1946 to 1981 has previously been documented.[4] From 1946 to the present, the name for the Muroc site changed several times. Table 1 shows the different names and the dates of change. Note that on 1 October 1958, NACA became the National Aeronautics and Space Administration (NASA). The formation of NASA from NACA was a result of the launch of the first earth satellite, Sputnik 1, on 4 October 1957 by the Union of Soviet Socialist Republics (U.S.S.R.). In addition to the NACA responsibilities, NASA had responsibility for the civilian space program.

The name changes during the early years, particularly 1946 to 1954, were an indication of the increasing number of both programs and people at the Muroc site. The maximum number of civil service personnel working at Muroc/Dryden was in the mid-1960s (669 in 1965).[6] In mid-1996, there were approximately 450 civil service employees and approximately that many contractor support personnel.‡ The name changes also reflect the increasing autonomy of the Muroc site. The three factors of increased programs, people and autonomy directly affected the working environment for the women in the engineering field.

The discussion that follows concerns the changes in the environment for the women in the engineering field at Muroc/Dryden. Only the NACA/NASA civil service women are discussed; records were not available for women who worked for contractors. During the early days at Muroc/Dryden, until about 1954, the women who worked as computers were treated as junior engineers both in the tasks they were assigned and in their working relationship with the male engineers. The data gathering and analysis

Table 1. - Muroc/Dryden Name Changes	
Date	**Name**
30 September 1946	NACA Muroc unit†††
7 September 1947	NACA Muroc Flight Test Unit[5]
14 November 1949	NACA High-Speed Flight Research Station (HSFRS)
1 July 1954	NACA High-Speed Flight Station (HSFS)
1 October 1958	NASA High-Speed Flight Station (HSFS)
27 September 1959	NASA Flight Research Center (FRC)
26 March 1976	NASA Hugh L. Dryden Flight Research Center (DFRC, Dryden)
1 October 1981	NASA Ames Research Center, Dryden Flight Research Facility (DFRF, Dryden)
1 March 1994	NASA Hugh L. Dryden Flight Research Center (DFRC, Dryden)

procedures before the age of digital computers was labor intensive. To provide a better understanding of the labor involved, typical instrumentation used on the X-series aircraft from the X-1 through the X-15† is shown in Appendix B. Also discussed in Appendix B is the data reduction technique for the Mach number position error curve for the historic first flight to exceed the speed of sound with the X-1 aircraft. A Mach number and altitude plot from an X-15 flight is also shown.

Women's Involvement from 1946 to the Early 1950s

The women and probably many of the men sent from Langley had volunteered for the assignments at the Muroc site. The length of the assignments varied considerably, anywhere from four months to two years with one year being the most common. Some of the engineers were borrowed on contract for one or two years from the other NACA laboratories (Ames or Lewis). The first two women (the

computers) assigned to the Muroc site can be seen in the group photograph taken in late 1946 (fig. 3). The policy at Langley at that time was to hire women with math degrees to be computers. Roxanah Yancey, who had a math degree, remained at the Muroc site until her retirement in 1973. Isabell Martin, who also had a math degree, had left the Muroc site by early 1947.

By October of 1947, 27 persons were working at the Muroc site. The group photograph (fig. 4) shows 24 persons, 4 of them women. Roxanah Yancey, Phyllis Rogers Actis and Dorothy Clift Hughes were the woman computers at that time. Naomi Wimmer was secretary to Walter (Walt) Williams, head of the NACA Muroc Flight Test Unit. An interesting aside is that 2 persons (Gerald Truszynski and Clyde Bailey) were not in the original photograph. Images from other photographs were pasted in to obtain this second group photograph. The original negatives are not available for either of these group photographs.

† This was a rocket-powered aircraft that was air-launched from a B-52 airplane. There were three X-15 aircraft flown between 1959 and 1968. The X-15 extended piloted flight to a maximum Mach number of 6.67 (4520 mph) and to a maximum altitude of 354,200 feet. It was the first aircraft to use thrusters for pitch, yaw, and roll control on the fringes of the atmosphere. Data collected from the various studies, including heating, materials, pressures, stability, and flight control, were important in the development of spacecraft as well as today's operational aircraft. Besides Hallion, *On the Frontier*, pp. 101-129, Milton O. Thompson, *At the Edge of Space: The X-15 Flight Program* (Washington, D.C.: Smithsonian Institution Press, 1992) and Wendell H. Stillwell, *X-15 Research Results* (Washington, D.C.: NASA SP-60, 1965) provide further information on this hypersonic aircraft and the flight research conducted with it.

Figure 3. Group photograph in front of the XS-1 and the B-29 (carrier airplane for the XS-1), late 1946. Standing from left to right: Charles Forsyth, Cloyce Matheny, Beverly Porter Brown, John Gardner, De E. Beeler, Roxanah Yancey, Walter Williams, Isabell Martin, and William (Bill) Aiken. Kneeling from left to right: Clyde Bailey, William Hampton, George Minalga, Joel R. (Bob) Baker and LeRoy Proctor, Jr. (NASA Photo E21428)

Figure 4. Group photograph in front of the B-29, October 1947. Standing left to right: Charles Hamilton, Milton McLaughlin, Joseph Vensel, Herbert Hoover, Roxanah Yancey, Hubert Drake, Phyllis Rogers Actis, Howard Lilly, Naomi C. Wimmer, Frank Hughes, Dorothy Clift Hughes, Arthur William (Bill) Vernon, Gerald Truszynski, Walter Williams, Clyde Bailey and Harold Goodman. Kneeling from left to right: LeRoy Proctor, Jr., Donald Borchers, Harold Nemecek, Elmer Bigg, John Gardner, De E. Beeler, John Mayer and Eugene Beckwith. (NASA Photo E21431)

The number of people at the NACA Muroc site almost doubled each year from 1947 to 1950. There were 40 persons in May of 1948, 60 in January of 1949, and 132 in January of 1950. The group photograph taken in 1950 (fig. 5) shows that the number of women had increased significantly from the four of 1947.

Until 1957, the single women and men could live in NACA dormitories on the base. The original dormitories, at least for

Figure 5. Group photograph in front of the NACA building, 1950. Roxanah Yancey is in the first row of women, third from the right. (NASA Photo E21429)

5

the women, were makeshift facilities. From December of 1946 to the spring of 1949, the women's dormitory appears to have been a series of different buildings. The following quotation[†] mentions several of the women's living areas:

> Upon arriving at Muroc in December 1946, Roxie began at Kerosene Flats (so named because of the heating method) what was to be a nomadic existence. From Kerosene Flats, she went to housing opened in the hospital area by the Air Force—then to the Air Force nurses' quarters, made available to Civil Service personnel for a limited time—next, to the "Guest House" for three days—and for 5 years, to the NACA Women's Dorm.

One of the buildings used by the women in the spring of 1949 was the Red Cross building at the South Base. This building was near the hangar NACA used until late 1948 (remembered as being approximately 500 ft away). The men could live in the Bachelor Officer Quarters (BOQ) but faced the possibility of being displaced by military men who needed a room for a night or more.

By 1948, the unsatisfactory conditions of the original dormitories and the work facilities were seriously affecting morale and making it difficult to recruit people. A dormitory was considered essential in the recruiting of single women (and important in the recruiting of single men) because of the remote location of the work site. The nearest town of any size was approximately 30 miles away. There was not a public transportation system, and most of the women did not own cars. (Some, like Roxanah Yancey, learned to drive after coming to Muroc.) Some of the women did live off the base and were riders in carpools from Mojave or Willow Springs (approximately 9 miles west of Rosamond). Figure 1 shows these town locations.

The women who lived on base were allowed after-hours and weekend use of a NACA vehicle, a Dodge carryall, which they named the Gray Ghost. The carryall

had been loaned to the Muroc site by the Ames Laboratory. The Gray Ghost apparently was a basic transportation vehicle; in other words, it was better than no car at all. Figure 6 is a photograph of Roxanah Yancey with the Gray Ghost. The living conditions at Muroc were bleak and the following three quotations give a feeling for the living and working conditions in 1947 and 1948. The first quotation is from Appendix A:

> Muroc in 1947. . . a land of plentiful sunshine, warm dry air, the wide open spaces with unlimited visibility and ceiling conditions. Muroc in 1947. . . a wind-swept, flat desert area with winds reaching 50 mph creating dust and sandstorms that reduce both visibility and ceiling conditions to 400 feet. An area capable of producing temperatures from 5° F to 115° F. Muroc in 1947. . . manbuilt structures that provided a bare minimum in living comfort by any standards of the day.[††]

The second quotation is from Richard Hallion's *On the Frontier*[7]:

> Muroc Air Force Base in early 1948 was not only remote, it was bleak. In December 1947, NACA's work came to a standstill as personnel scrambled away to celebrate the holidays in more appealing sections of the country. Indeed, one reason for the impressive amount of work that got done might have been sociological: there was little else to do. Even by automobile, a trip to Los Angeles was a chore; without one, the remaining choice was the afternoon Stage Lines[†††] bus that left Muroc for Los Angeles at about 5 p.m. The voyager had to spend the night in Los Angeles and take another bus back the next evening. Word about the discomforts of Muroc soon spread within the NACA labs, making recruitment very difficult.

The third quotation was actually made about the living conditions in the summer

[†] This is from Appendix A in the Personalities section of the 10th anniversary *X-PRESS*. This includes brief profiles of each of the 10 people who were at Muroc for the first supersonic flight in 1947 and were still working at the High Speed Flight Station in 1957. Roxie refers to Roxanah Yancey, the only woman in the group of 10. Brief job descriptions accompany the profiles for the 9 men.

[††] This was written by De E. Beeler and continues with a discussion of the importance of the X-1 aircraft tests as the reason the people stayed. He also refers to the housing facilities in a later paragraph as "equivalent to high-type stables."

[†††] The actual name was the Trona Stage. The route for this bus originated in Trona, which is near Death Valley (between China Lake Naval Weapons Center and the northwest edge of Searles Lake shown in fig. 1), and ended at the Greyhound Bus station in Los Angeles. The following day, the bus would return to Trona, according to the recollections of Mary Little Kuhl on 5 April 1994.

† The tests involved removing the propeller from the P-51, towing it to between 25,000 and 30,000 feet with a P-61 (twin-engine Black Widow), cutting loose at the desired altitude, and then diving to a glide landing. Engineers compared the data from these full-scale tests with data from a P-51 wind-tunnel model (with no propellers).

†† Tut Hedgepeth, a woman computer, remembered her starting salary in 1948 as being $2,300 (interview on 28 October 1992). Walt Williams, head of the Muroc unit, remembered his starting salary as $2,000 in 1940, with a subsequent raise to $2,600. By the late 1940s, he was earning $3,200 (interview on 17 September 1993).

Figure 6. Roxanah Yancey with the NACA Dodge carryall named the Gray Ghost, late 1940s or early 1950s. (NASA Photo E96 4340331)

of 1944 when NACA Ames Laboratory (near San Francisco, California) was conducting tests on the P-51 Mustang airplane†:

> A place in which these daring tests could be made in privacy was desired, and the Army offered the use of its Muroc Flight Test Base in southern California. This is an isolated military reservation in the Mohave Desert [sic]—a remote, treeless, desolate terrain which offered a landing field about five miles in diameter.[8]

Perhaps the memories from these tests were the reason recruits for Muroc came primarily from the NACA Langley (Hampton, Virginia) and Lewis Laboratories (Cleveland, Ohio).

Another factor that increased the recruiting difficulties was that during the summer of 1947 Langley decided to establish the test team permanently as the Muroc Flight Test Unit. This meant the staff no longer received the $3 to $4 per diem as employees on temporary duty. Those who chose to leave were paid for their return to Langley.[9] To put the per diem amount in perspective, assume an annual salary of $2,400.†† The $2,400 per year would be an average of $200 per month. For a 30-day month, the $3 per diem would be $90 extra and the $4 per diem would be $120 extra. This amount would indeed be a significant supplement to an income.

The NACA decided that in order to recruit people to work at the Muroc site, it was necessary to improve the dormitories and the work facilities. The NACA Ames Laboratory provided personnel, including model makers, to support the construction work on the new dormitories and other NACA Muroc facilities (existing buildings being modified). The shops and offices were completed in November of 1948 and the dormitories in the spring of 1949. An aerial photograph taken in 1951 [fig. 7 (a)] shows the location of the NACA work site with respect to the women's dormitory. The NACA work site was at this location from late 1948 until mid-1954. Note how close the work site is to the runway.[†] Figure 7 (b) shows a closer view of the women's dormitory.[††] While the women's dormitory remained at the South Base, the men's dormi-

Figure 7. Aerial views of the women's dormitory at the south base. (a. above) July 1951; women's dormitory with respect to NACA site (NASA Photo E499). (b. below) Late 1949 or early 1950 showing the area around the women's dormitory.

[†] The runway is 30 degrees from being in an east-west direction. Using the standard convention of north being 0 degrees and south at 180 degrees, the east end of the runway is 60 degrees from the north and the west end, 240 degrees from the north. The hangars are on the north side of the runway.

[††] Some of the photographs used in this document came from original NACA negatives and some were from copies of photographs. The NACA Photo Log, a negative summary, includes negative number, a few descriptive words, name of person requesting the photograph, date when the photograph was taken and date completed. The date completed corresponds to when the prints were available. Some of the early negatives listed in the NACA Photo Log have disappeared. The original negative for this photograph was probably from a series of five aerial view negatives, none of which are in the negative file. These negatives did not have dates for when the photographs were taken, but the completion dates for the negatives preceding and following the aerial view negatives were 8 June 1950 and 26 July 1950, respectively.

men's dormitory cost $3.69 every two weeks for a double room and $6.00 for a single room. The dormitory cost, which was deducted from the bi-weekly paycheck, also included janitor service. For comparison, a one bedroom, one bathroom apartment with a kitchen and a living room rented for $75 to $100 per month in Lancaster in 1956. (Recollections of Terry Larson on 11 May 1994.) The women's dormitory in 1952 and 1953, which had only single rooms, cost $3.46 weekly ($6.92 every two weeks). The dormitory cost, which included maid (janitor) service, was deducted from the paycheck. In 1954, the starting salary for an engineer graduating from college with a bachelor degree was $3410. (Recollections of Harriet Smith on 13 June 1996.)

tory was at the North Base (fig. 2), an approximately 8 mile drive. The men's dormitory, because of its distance from the base eating areas, had a kitchen and a cook to prepare meals.†

The one-story, two-wing women's dormitory had room for 10 and was near the base cafeteria, chapel, and theater (fig. 7). One wing had four rooms and the other had six rooms. Each wing had a bathroom. The bathroom in the six-room wing had two shower stalls; the one in the four-room wing had one shower stall. The communal living area included a kitchen, complete with stove and refrigerator; a living room that also contained the dining room table; and a laundry room containing one washing machine and one dryer. Each of the women had an evaporative cooler in her room.

(a) Front door entrance. (NASA Photo E96 43403-8)

(b) Parking area and exterior side view. Gray Ghost (Dodge carryall) in background. Evaporative coolers are mounted at windows. (NASA Photo E96 43403-7)

(c) View of bedroom. (NASA Photo E52)

(d) View of dining area. (NASA Photo E50)

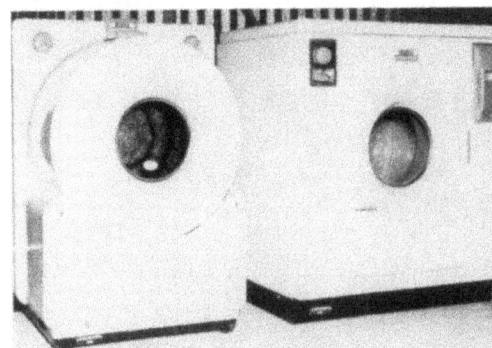

(e) Washer and dryer in laundry room. (NASA Photo E51)

(f) View of kitchen stove. (NASA Photo E49)

Figure 8. Interior and exterior views of women's dormitory, 1949 or early 1950s.

Because the humidity is usually low, the evaporative coolers were quite effective in providing cooling. However, they made the room and everything in it very damp which is why they are also called swamp coolers. Figure 8[†] shows exterior and interior views of the NACA woman's dormitory. The front porch [fig. 8 (a)] faced the street. The evaporative coolers are seen in Figure 8 (b). Note the Gray Ghost in the background. The minimal landscaping seen in the photographs was typical for the South Base at that time. The most extensive landscaping, a few trees and some grass, was for the base headquarters [fig. 7 (a)]. A bedroom, the dining area, the laundry room and the kitchen stove are shown in Figures 8 (c) through 8 (f), respectively. Note the fire extinguisher by the kitchen stove [fig. 8 (f)] and by the front door [fig. 8 (a)].

The late 1940s saw increased flight activity, and more women computers (self-dubbed the Muroc Computers) were needed at the NACA Muroc Flight Test Unit. A call went out to the NACA Langley, Lewis and Ames laboratories for more women computers. In response to that call, Lilly Ann Bajus, Dorothy (Dottie) Crawford and Gertrude (Trudy) Wilken from Lewis and Angel Dunn, Mary (Tut) Hedgepeth, Mary Little and Beverly Smith from Langley came to NACA Muroc. Figure 9 shows some of these woman in a group photograph taken at the work site in late 1948[††] (probably November or December). The women computers in the photograph are Roxanah Yancey, Mary (Tut) Hedgepeth, Dorothy Crawford Roth, Dorothy Clift Hughes, Lilly Ann Bajus, Gertrude (Trudy) Wilken Valentine, Angel Dunn and Emily Stephens. Also photographed were Jane Collons who worked in procurement, and Leona Corbett who, at least when she first came, was secretary to the head of the unit at Muroc, Walter (Walt) Williams.

Most of the women who worked at the NACA Muroc site in the late 1940s had left by the early 1950s. Three women— Roxanah, Mary Little and Leona—remained working at the NACA site until their retirements. Leona was working in the personnel branch (head of the Civil

[†] The photographs in figures 6 and 8 were copied from photographs belonging to Mary Little Kuhl.

[††] There was no date in the NACA Photo Log negative files, but the negative was one of 115 listed without dates between negatives dated as taken 13 October 1949 and 13 December 1949. The 1949 date does not agree with what some of the women remembered. Some of those in the photograph were not at Muroc in 1949. The most credible recollection (of Mary Little Kuhl on 20 November 1992) placed the snow as occurring during 1948. Even though the winters in the area are cold, big snows—indeed, any snow—are infrequent (years apart) and remembered for a long time.

Figure 9. Group photograph of women by snowman, late 1948. Standing left to right: Mary (Tut) Hedgepeth, Lilly Ann Bajus, Roxanah Yancey, Emily Stephens, Jane Collons, Leona Corbett and Angel Dunn. Kneeling left to right: Dorothy Crawford Roth, Dorothy Clift Hughes and Gertrude (Trudy) Wilken Valentine. Walter Williams is looking out the door. (NASA Photo E212)

† Mary is mentioned in the profile for Richard Payne in the PERSONALITIES section of the 10th anniversary *X-PRESS* in Appendix A.

†† These comments are from recollections of Tut Hedgepeth on 28 October 1992. To provide a feeling for living expenses, Walt Williams recalled on 17 September 1993 not only the salary figures given in the note on page 7 but the fact that in 1949 he bought a new Oldsmobile model 98 for $2,800. He considered a Lincoln Continental, but it cost $3,000. He remembers thinking "that was a lot for a car." By picking up his new car in Michigan, he saved $300. Terry Larson recalled on 11 May 1994 that his starting salary in 1953 after his graduation from college was $3,500. At that time, gasoline cost 28 to 29 cents per gallon, bread was 15 cents per loaf, bowling 25 cents a line and movies also cost a quarter.

Service Board of Examiners) when she retired in late 1966. There were many reasons the women left. Two returned to their former worksite (Emily to Langley and Lilly Ann to Lewis). Some left when they had children. For example, Mary M. Payne, also a woman computer from 1948 to 1951, came to NACA Muroc as a bride and quit work when her first child was born.† Some of the women married men who worked at NACA Muroc or in the local area and left when their husbands did. One interesting story about this concerns Beverly Smith. It seems that the women previewed the records of any new arrivals. Beverly was around 5 ft 9 in. to 5 ft 10 in. tall. One of the new arrivals was Larry Smith, who was single and 6 ft 2 in. tall. The women decided he should be the one for Beverly to marry, and, as it happened, she did marry him.

Some women came to work at the Muroc site because their husbands did. Two of these women were Angel Dunn and Mary (Tut) Hedgepeth, both from NACA Langley. Angel and her husband left the NACA Muroc unit after a few years. Tut arrived in November of 1948 with her husband, who started and worked for several years in the photography lab at the

NACA Muroc unit. Tut left the NACA Muroc unit in 1953 to work for the Air Force on the base. She started work at NACA Langley in 1948 for an annual salary of $2300 after graduation from college.†† Her father said that was more money than he had ever earned in a year (but he did put three daughters through college).

Recruiting visits and word of mouth were also useful in finding woman computers. Beverly Swanson Cothren, who worked at Langley, was recruited by Roxanah Yancey in 1949. When she first came, there was so much work that for the first six weeks she also worked weekends. Employees were also sought from the California colleges and from the local area. Harriet DeVries Smith began working with the women computers in the summer of 1952 as a co-op student. following a recruiting visit by De E. Beeler, one of the early Muroc employees mentioned in Appendix A. After graduation she returned as an engineer. She had some problems being accepted as an engineer for a year or two because of her previous work with the women computers. One of the men engineers, in particular, wanted her to continue to work as a woman computer. Word of mouth was how Betty Love, who

a. Viewed from the runway direction, late 1940s. (NASA Photo E51 503)

Figure 10. Aerial views of NACA site at the south base.

lived in the local area, heard of positions for woman computers. She applied and began working as a woman computer in 1952.[10]

Figure 10 shows two aerial views of the NACA Muroc site. Figure 10 (a), a photograph taken in the late 1940s, shows the site from the runway direction. Figure 10 (b), which was taken in 1951,[†] shows

fly to the NACA Muroc unit only when he was scheduled to pilot the X-1. Between test flights, he would fly a C-47 aircraft back to Langley (a 2 day trip each way of 6 to 7 hours each day).[11]

The aircraft being tested, such as the X-1 and the D-558, were at the leading edge of technology. The information and data obtained from these aircraft would

Figure 10b. Viewed from buildings to runway, July 1951. (NASA Photo E501)

the NACA work site from a different direction. The photograph shows the paved runway ending at the edge of Rogers Dry Lake.[††] Note that the airplanes at the Republic hangar had to taxi on the road to get to the runway.

Figures 7, 8 (a), 8 (b) and 10 also show the desert vegetation and indicate how different the climate was for the people from the east coast. The climate and the remote location were an unpleasant surprise to many people. In addition, family and old friends had often been left behind. Many people only stayed for their defined tour of duty (such as 4 months or 2 years). In fact, the first reaction of a new arrival was often to begin working on a plan to leave the area as soon as possible. One of the pilots, Herbert Hoover, would

significantly affect the future of aviation. For some, working on these aircraft was reason enough to stay. One example of the leading-edge data obtained is the noseboom pressure traces (fig. 11) from the historic flight of the X-1 airplane flown by Charles E. Yeager on 14 October 1947. These pressure traces are a record of the Mach jump from the first piloted airplane flight to exceed the speed of sound (exceed a Mach number of 1). The abrupt change in the pressure traces means that the bow shock wave of the aircraft has passed over the flush static pressure orifices on the noseboom and that the airplane is traveling faster than a Mach number of 1.[†††]

Translating film traces, such as those in Figure 11, into usable engineering data

† Figures 7 (a) and 10 (b) are from a sequence of nine aerial photographs taken, according to the NACA Photo Log, on 12 July 1951.

†† The Rogers Dry lakebed is part of the runway system (with Rosamond Dry Lake also available for landings but primarily as a backup). The paved runways are preferred because the lakebed is very dusty. Occasionally, there has actually been enough rain that the Rogers lakebed has been wet and unusable. Some flight programs, such as that for the X-15, could only land on Rogers lakebed. When heavy rain precluded its use, the programs were delayed until the lakebed dried out.

††† The pressure traces are for the impact pressure, q_c, and the static pressure, p. The total head pressure, P_T, is the sum of these pressures ($P_T = q_c + p$). P_T remains unaffected by the passage of the shock. The impact pressure is the pressure differential between the static pressure and the total pressure. Thus, when the static pressure "jumps," the impact pressure will "jump" an equal amount (the same pressure change) in the opposite direction. The amount of movement of the two traces is different because of sensitivity differences (amount of pressure change per inch of movement) between the two traces. After applying calibrations (discussed in Appendix B), the change in pressure for the two traces is equal and opposite.

was one of the tasks of the women computers. Other tasks included plotting calibration curves and data and calculating for the fuel usage, weight and balance, and center of gravity position for the airplanes. Translating the traces on the oscillograph film into usable data required considerable effort. Figure 12 shows a roll of a photo-sensitive paper copy of the oscillograph film, and two of the tools used in the data analysis process, a film scale and a slide rule. The horizontal traces on the oscillograph film were either reference traces or data traces. The vertical lines were the time scale. A film scale was used to read the difference (delta) between a data trace and its reference trace at the desired time. This process was commonly referred to as reading the film. The engineering value for each delta was then read

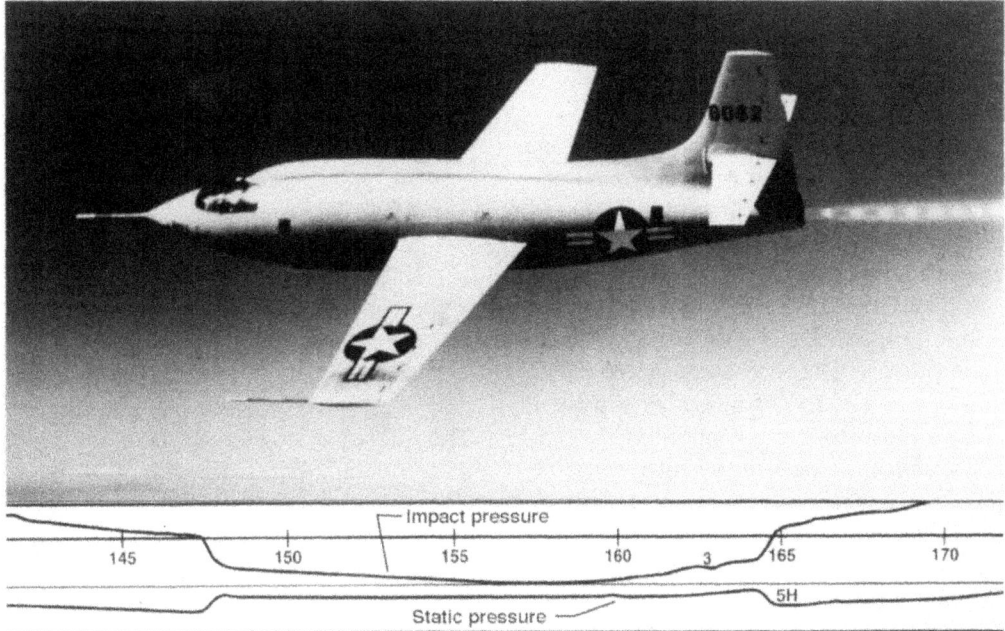

Figure 11. XS-1 and film pressure traces from first airplane flight to exceed the speed of sound. Flown by Charles Yeager on 14 October 1947.

Figure 12. Engineers (left to right) Jack Fischel, Arthur Gardner and John Rogers with a copy of an oscillograph film, film scale and slide rule, about 1950. (NASA Photo E92 11191-2)

13

from the corresponding calibration plot. After the engineering values were obtained, the desired parameters were calculated using the appropriate tools (slide rule, mechanical calculator, standard atmosphere tables, sine and cosine tables, etc.). This procedure is discussed in more detail in Appendix B where the data workup and plot are presented for the indicated and corrected Mach number comparison from the flights leading to and including the first piloted flight to exceed the speed of sound.

Appendix B also includes a brief discussion about the film recorder system, the tools used by the women computers and engineers, and a time history plot showing the altitude, velocity, dynamic pressure, and Mach number for an X-15 airplane flight. The X-15 was the last X-series airplane to use oscillograph film for the primary data recording system. The X-15 was also the first X-series airplane to use a pulse code modulation (PCM) system for the data recording system.[†]

The engineers did some film reading, calculations, and plotting, but most of this work was done by the computers. This tedious and time-consuming work required a great deal of patience. Men were not thought to have the patience to do this work, so almost all computers were women. The following quotation briefly describes the work involved in reading film.

> Though equipment changed over the years and most computers eventually found themselves programming and operating electronic computers, as well as doing other data processing tasks, being a computer initially meant long hours with a slide rule, hunched over illuminated light boxes measuring line traces from grainy and obscure strips of oscillograph film. Computers suffered terrible eyestrain and those who didn't begin by wearing glasses did so after a few years.[12]

The quotation mistakenly mentions a slide rule; in fact, a film scale with marked divisions to 0.02 inches was used to read the film. However, slide rules and also mechanical calculators were used for doing calculations before the days of digital computers.[††]

[†] The checkout flights for the PCM system were flown on one of the F-104 aircraft at Dryden. When the system was deemed ready, it was installed in the X-15 #3 aircraft. The first X-15 flight with the PCM system occurred on 26 April 1967. Unfortunately, on 15 November 1967 (the eighth flight using the PCM system), the X-15 #3 aircraft was destroyed in an accident that also resulted in the death of the pilot. In a PCM system, the signal for a measurement, for example from a pressure transducer or a thermocouple, is sampled and then encoded into a binary number whose value is proportional to the amplitude of the signal. The measurements from several transducers are obtained by taking a sample from each transducer in sequence and encoding the measurement from each transducer in the same sequence. The encoded signals are sent in a sequel stream (say, pressure 1, pressure 2, temperature 1, pressure 3, temperature 2, etc.) in which the signals in each sequential stream have a common sampling rate per second. Some commonly used sampling rates are 20 samples per second (sps), 40 sps, and 200 sps. The sequel output of the PCM system could be sent to a tape recorder on the airplane or radioed to a ground station, or both. The output signal from the PCM is then separated into the individual measurements and translated into engineering units, for example pressures or temperatures. A PCM system for a small aircraft typically handles 50 to 200 measurements while a PCM system for a large aircraft could handle from 400 to 2,000 measurements. For details about PCM systems, see O. J. Strock, *Telemetry Computer Systems, the New Generation* (Instrument Society of America, 1988).

[††] The calculators used were Friden automatic calculators. The users named the calculators "Galloping Gerties" because of their motion when in use. Note the pads under them in Figure 13. These pads were supposed to cushion the motion.

a. Mechanical calculators, Fridens, are seen on desks on the left side. Woman at center desk with lamp is reading film traces. Clockwise from desk on right side: Roxanah Yancey, Geraldine Mayer, Mary (Tut) Hedgepeth, Emily Stephens, John Mayer, Gertrude (Trudy) Valentine, and Dorothy Clift Hughes. (NASA Photo E53)

Figure 13. Two views of women computers at work, spring 1949.

† Both a calibration plot and a time history plot are shown in Appendix B. The time history plot is for an X-15 flight.

†† There was no date in the Dryden negative files but these were 2 of the 67 negatives listed without dates between the negatives dated as taken 10 October 1949 and 13 October 1949. The October date does not agree with the memories of the women. They said it was taken earlier in 1949. The month and year of the claendar on the wall in Figure 13 (b) is not legible. However, the calendar is for a 30-day month that began on a Friday and ends on a Saturday. For 1949, this turns out to be April. The clothing is consistent with the late spring or early summer, so I decided to date the photograph as spring. The work environment for the women computers was tightly controlled. The women were expected to be at their desks working with very little time allowed for breaks. One accepted break was to get coffee, which required walking through the hanger. Some of the women who weren't coffee drinkers became coffee drinkers after starting work because going for coffee gave them a chance to get away from their desks. For special events, such as the landing of X-planes, they were allowed to open the blinds at the window and watch the landing. Going outside to watch the event was considered too long a break. (Recollections of Beverly Cothren, Harriet Smith and Betty Love on 13 June 1996 about the work envoronment.) The work environment for the men may have also been tightly controlled but I suspect there was much more leeway from some of the tales I have heard of the early days.

††† I could not find the negative for this photograph. An attempt to enlarge the area of the negative used for the photograph in Figure 13 (b) was unsuccessful; the Dryden photo lab was unable to make a legible print from such an enlargement. The women in the smaller photograph were identified (left to right) as Teal Hildebrand (secretary at the Western Coordination office of the NACA in Los Angeles), Dorothy Crawford Roth, Trudy Wilken Valentine, Lilly Ann Bajus, Jane Collons, Emily Stephens (probably) and Mary Payne.

Other sources of eyestrain were plotting and reading values from plots; for example, calibration of X-15 time history plots.† The X-15 time history plots were used by engineers and probably some of the woman computers to obtain the Mach number, velocity, altitude, and dynamic pressure for the required times. Figure 13 shows two views of "Muroc computers" at work during what appears to have been the spring of 1949.†† Figure 13 (a) shows the calculators on the left side of the

any available opening during high winds or sandstorms. Also note the photographs on the support beam. The middle photograph shows seven women in slacks and wearing parachutes.††† They were probably dressed to ride in the airplane (probably a Douglas DC-3) behind them in the photograph.

The working environment for the women computers during the early days at the Muroc site was influenced by several

Figure 13b. Note cover on Friden calculator. Left side, front to back, Mary (Tut) Hedgepeth, John Mayer and Emily Stephens. Right side, front to back. Lilly Ann Bajus, Roxanah Yancey, Gertrude (Trudy) Valentine (behind Roxanah) and Ilene Alexander. (NASA Photo E54)

desks. The two women at the center desks in the back are working with film. Trudy is reading film traces from a photosensitive paper copy of the film. Dorothy is looking at a roll of film, probably to find the time segment she wants to read. Figure 13 (b) shows Lilly Ann working with the data sheets used to record the numbers from film deflection to final value. Note the assortment of curves on Roxanah's desk and the cover on the Friden automatic calculator. As well as looking nice, the covers helped protect the Fridens from sand that blew into the buildings through

factors. Two of these were the small numbers of people working there and the remote location. The small numbers meant that everyone was well-known by all in the group. This familiarity fostered a strong team spirit that resulted in people helping wherever they were needed. The remote location strengthened this team spirit because the activities after work involved the same people.

Another factor that strongly influenced the work environment for the woman computers during the mid-to-late 1940s was a consequence of World War II (WW II). In November of 1942, NACA Langley announced that women would be hired for "vital war work" and hold jobs formerly only held by men.[13] During the war, women college students were encouraged to enter engineering. The following quotation, from an Iowa State University alumni newspaper, was entitled "WW II Propels Women Into Engineering." The Ames mentioned is the location of Iowa State College (presently Iowa State University).

"Nearly half of the students enrolled in the college's aeronautical engineering department in 1943 were women. They were part of a unique training program sponsored by Curtiss Wright Corporation, an aircraft manufacturer. "In 10 months time, we had been 'spoon fed' the equivalent of two years of engineering, so that we would be able to replace the junior engineers that were being drafted to serve in WW II," said Jean (Nickerson) Patterson of Clinton, Iowa. "We were there for such a short time that you may never have heard of us."

The 97 women came to Ames from 22 states to be among the 711 "Curtiss Wright Engineering Cadettes" studying on seven campuses. Most were college juniors, majoring in everything from chemistry to art. For 40 hours each week, they attended classes and labs in

math, mechanics, aerodynamics, aircraft structures, drafting, and manufacturing materials and processes. After completing the training, they worked for Curtiss Wright in St. Louis, Dayton, or Buffalo. The program had an immense impact on their lives, Patterson said. Following the war, many completed their degrees and most "used some form of their Curtiss Wright training in their professional lives."[14]

A photograph included with the article shows two women welding with a caption saying, "As part of their 10-month wartime training program, the Curtiss Wright Cadettes mastered the welding torch in preparation for work as junior engineers in the aircraft industry."

The tasks for the woman computers at the NACA Muroc site were certainly different from those of the Curtiss Wright Cadettes, but both groups were working as junior engineers. This meant that the computers worked closely with the engineers and were often co-authors on technical reports. This working environment existed until the early 1950s.

Working Environment Change in the Early 1950s

Several changes occurred in the early 1950s that affected the working environment for the women. The changes were good for the Muroc unit but not necessarily for the women, especially the women

Figure 14. NACA's X-series fleet in the late 1940s or early 1950s (from left): Douglas D-558-2 Skyrocket, Douglas D-558-1 Skystreak, Bell X-5, Bell X-1, Convair XF-92A, Northrop X-4. (NASA Photo E145)

computers. These changes, discussed in more detail in the following paragraphs, were the increase in number of aircraft being tested, organizational changes, autonomy from Langley, the move to a larger building and the increase in science and engineering graduates because of the GI Bill.

The increase in the number of aircraft being tested directly translated into a need for more people. Figure 14 shows the aircraft being tested in the late 1940s or early 1950s. The Xes painted on the sides

there were no women in the ground support crews. The computers, research engineers, and administration, reproduction and library personnel were in the building seen on the right that is connected by a walkway to the hangar. Figure 10 shows this building labeled as the NACA Office Building. The machine shop was in the narrow building (actually a lean-to) attached to the hangar on the left side. The instrumentation people were in a building across the street, and Figure 7 (a) shows the site where the radar people were located.

Figure 15. Flight support required for D-558-2 air launch flight, taken 17 January 1954. D-558-2 (white airplane in front), two F-86 chase aircraft and B-29 (carrier aircraft). Scott Crossfield, D-558-2 pilot, standing at nose of D-558-2. (NASA Photo E1152)

of the aircraft (all except the Bell X-5; most noticeable on the Bell X-1, XF-92A and X-4) in the photograph were used for one of the experiments to photographically document the attitude during landing.† After the flight, the attitude of the aircraft during landing was determined from the photographs. Figure 15 shows the aircraft and ground crew support needed for one flight on the air-launched D-558-2 airplane. It is interesting to note (and not easily seen) that each of the F-86 aircraft has a man sitting in the cockpit. Also note that

The increase in people (because of the number of aircraft being tested) changed the small, intimate group working environment and led to less interaction between the women computers and the engineers. (In May 1948 there were approximately 40 people; in July 1954, 250 people, and in 1960, 408 people.) This change can be inferred from organizational charts for 1948, 1954 and 1960.[15]

The organization chart from February 1 to July 1, 1948 shows R. Yancey as the

Head Computer reporting to the Head of Engineering. The Project Engineers for each of the six airplane projects also reported to the Head of Engineering. Each of the six airplane projects have separate "boxes" with the names of the project engineer, engineer, and computers assigned to the project. Several of the boxes, especially for the computers, do not have names. Computers D. Clift and M. M. Payne were assigned to the X-1 #1 aircraft, P. Rogers to the X-1 #2, and H. Wall to the D-558-1 #2 aircraft. By the early to mid-1950s, the women computers began working in a computer group that was supervised by Roxanah Yancey. The organization chart for July 1954 shows "boxes" for the different functions but no names. The computers, now in an organization called Computing Service, constituted a separate function in the Research Division. The Research Division also included the Stability and Control Branch, Loads Branch, and Performance Branch. The next organizational chart is for July 1960. The Research Division still existed, but the computers were now in the Simulation and Computation Branch of the Data Systems Division. Thus, the change for the computers from 1948 to 1960 was from working directly with the engineers to forming a service organization in a different division.

Another change, which also had a significant effect on the working environment for the women in the engineering field, was that in March 1954, the NACA High-Speed Flight Research Station (HSFRS) became the NACA High-Speed Flight Station (HSFS). The HSFS was now autonomous, which meant that Langley was no longer responsible for management or staffing. This autonomy resulted in a change in the technical background of the women in the computer group. Most

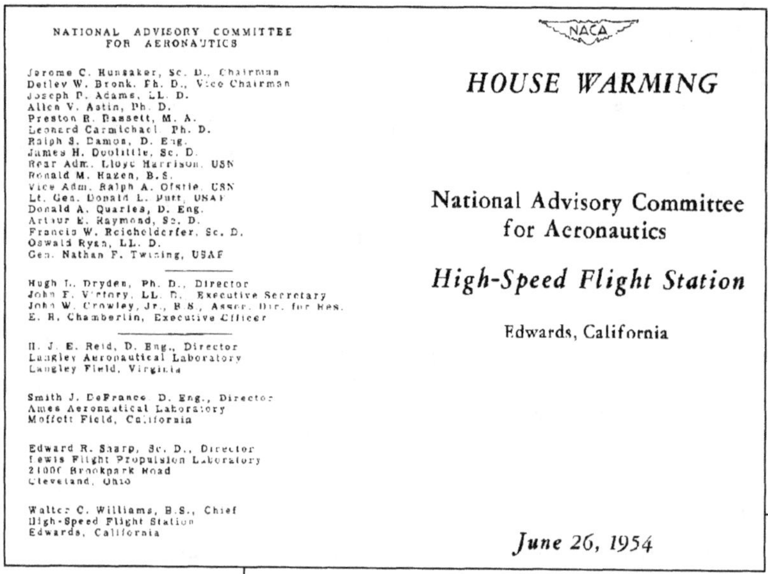

NATIONAL ADVISORY COMMITTEE
FOR AERONAUTICS

Jerome C. Hunsaker, Sc. D., Chairman
Detlev W. Bronk, Ph. D., Vice Chairman
Joseph P. Adams, LL. D.
Allen V. Astin, Ph. D.
Preston R. Bassett, M. A.
Leonard Carmichael, Ph. D.
Ralph S. Damon, D. Eng.
James H. Doolittle, Sc. D.
Rear Adm. Lloyd Harrison, USN
Ronald M. Hazen, B. S.
Vice Adm. Ralph A. Ofstie, USN
Lt. Gen. Donald L. Putt, USAF
Donald A. Quarles, D. Eng.
Arthur E. Raymond, Sc. D.
Francis W. Reichelderfer, Sc. D.
Oswald Ryan, LL. D.
Gen. Nathan F. Twining, USAF

Hugh L. Dryden, Ph. D., Director
John F. Victory, LL. D., Executive Secretary
John W. Crowley, Jr., B. S., Assoc. Dir. for Res.
E. H. Chamberlin, Executive Officer

H. J. E. Reid, D. Eng., Director
Langley Aeronautical Laboratory
Langley Field, Virginia

Smith J. DeFrance, D. Eng., Director
Ames Aeronautical Laboratory
Moffett Field, California

Edward R. Sharp, Sc. D., Director
Lewis Flight Propulsion Laboratory
21000 Brookpark Road
Cleveland, Ohio

Walter C. Williams, B.S., Chief
High-Speed Flight Station
Edwards, California

NACA

HOUSE WARMING

National Advisory Committee
for Aeronautics

High-Speed Flight Station

Edwards, California

June 26, 1954

Front and back cover of announcement. (Ilford print)

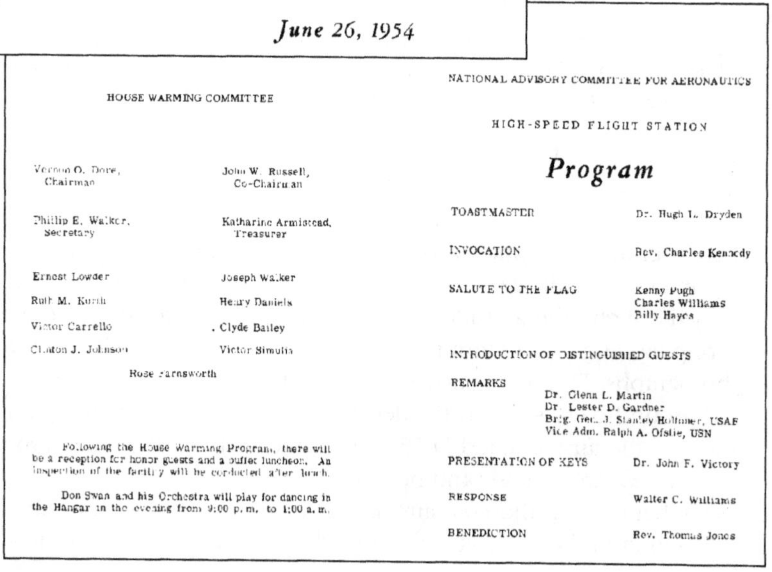

HOUSE WARMING COMMITTEE

Vernon O. Dore, Chairman	John W. Russell, Co-Chairman
Phillip E. Walker, Secretary	Katharine Armistead, Treasurer
Ernest Lowder	Joseph Walker
Ruth M. Korth	Henry Daniels
Victor Carrello	Clyde Bailey
Clinton J. Johnson	Victor Simulis

Rose Farnsworth

Following the House Warming Program, there will be a reception for honor guests and a buffet luncheon. An inspection of the facility will be conducted after lunch.

Don Swan and his Orchestra will play for dancing in the Hangar in the evening from 9:00 p. m. to 1:00 a. m.

NATIONAL ADVISORY COMMITTEE FOR AERONAUTICS

HIGH-SPEED FLIGHT STATION

Program

TOASTMASTER	Dr. Hugh L. Dryden
INVOCATION	Rev. Charles Kennedy
SALUTE TO THE FLAG	Kenny Pugh Charles Williams Billy Hayes
INTRODUCTION OF DISTINGUISHED GUESTS	
REMARKS	Dr. Glenn L. Martin Dr. Lester D. Gardner Brig. Gen. J. Stanley Holtoner, USAF Vice Adm. Ralph A. Ofstie, USN
PRESENTATION OF KEYS	Dr. John F. Victory
RESPONSE	Walter C. Williams
BENEDICTION	Rev. Thomas Jones

Inside pages of announcement. (Ilford print)

Figure 16. Announcement for House Warming Party held June 26, 1954 for new building.

Figure 17. Group photograph in front of the new building, main base, 1954. (NASA Photo E33718)

of the women assigned from Langley had math degrees. Most of the computers hired from the local area by the HSFRS and the HSFS did not have college degrees. This change led to the working assignments becoming more routine.

Also in June 1954, the HSFS personnel (now numbering 250 people) and airplanes moved from the South Base into a new, larger building on the main base. This structure, Building 4800, has been added to over the years and is still in use. To celebrate the move into the new building, a housewarming party, including a band for dancing, was held in one of the two hangars of the new complex. Figure 16 shows an announcement for the party. This document was an approximately 8- by 10-inch sheet that was folded to make an outside cover and two inside pages. The upper left shows the front and back of the cover and the lower right shows the inside two pages. Figure 17 shows a group photograph taken in 1954 in front of the new building. As can be seen by comparing Figures 5 and 17, the new building was considerably larger than the old one. The increase in office space meant that the women computers and engineers no

longer sat close to each other, or in other words, were separated from each other.

The last change that occurred during the late 1940s and early 1950s resulted from the end of World War II in 1945 and the introduction of the GI Bill. The GI Bill, passed shortly after the armistice, paid the tuition for the GIs who wanted to attend college. The GIs also received some money for living expenses. When they began graduating, men with science and engineering degrees were available for hire. The shortage of men with science and engineering degrees no longer existed, so the need for women to work as junior engineers was no longer there.

The end result of these changes was that the interaction between the women computers and engineers decreased. The women computers had depended on the engineers to provide the opportunity to be co-authors. In effect, the engineers provided guidance and direction for the women's careers. The decreasing interaction between the women computers and the engineers meant that, in general, this guidance and direction no longer existed; that the women computers were no longer co-authors on reports; and that there were fewer opportunities for women, even with degrees, to work in the technical engineering areas. The status of the women computers had changed from being, in effect, junior engineers who worked closely with the engineers to being part of a service organization with almost no direct interaction with the engineers. Because of the difference in the task, the women computers who began working after 1954 are not included in the discussions here. All the women computers listed as co-authors of reports began working at Muroc in 1952 or earlier.

Women Authors from 1949 to 1960

From 1950 to 1960, four women engineers worked at the Muroc unit. Two of them, Joan Childs Dahlen and Harriet DeVries Smith, were authors of NACA reports. Two of them, Anne Baldwin and Bertha Ryan began working in the unit around 1960. Anne worked only a short time at the unit (probably from late 1959 or early 1960 until early 1962) and was not an author on a report. Bertha worked at the unit from 1960 until 1966 – 1967 and produced two reports. Joan Childs was the first woman to write a technical report at the Muroc site. The report, NACA RM L52K13b, published in 1953, was about the stability characteristics of the Bell X-5 airplane.[16] Joan Childs, who had an engineering degree, started as a computer. When Walt Williams (chief of the NACA unit at Muroc) learned about her engineering degree, he began the process to have her reclassified. Because of his efforts, she was classified as an engineer and assigned to the engineering group.[17] She was at the Muroc site approximately two to three years, married an engineer, Theodore Dahlen, who also worked at the Muroc site, and left when he did. Harriet DeVries began working at the Muroc site in the summer of 1952 as a co-op student.[†] After graduation from college, she returned as an engineer and worked in the engineering field until 1983 when she transferred to a congressional staff position.

The women computers were co-authors on reports primarily from 1948 to 1952. During this period, 11 were co-authors. In 1957 and 1958, three more woman computers were co-authors. The reports from 1948 to 1958 were about experiments on the X-1, X-3,[††] X-5, D-558, and B-52 airplanes. The number of computers as co-authors was determined by looking through a card file of reports by Muroc/Dryden authors. The computers were always the last author listed on multiple author reports (usually two or three authors). During the period from 1946 to 1954, there were 29 woman computers whom I was able to identify.[†††] Appendix C contains the names of the women identified as being computers and co-authors from 1946 to 1954.

Work Environment Changes in the 1960s

The next change in the hiring and job requirements for women occurred during the early-to-mid-1960s. This change was caused by the development of digital computers and the need for people with college degrees to program them. One of the new people hired to work with the digital computers (at that time changing from an IBM 650 drum computer to an IBM 704 that used vacuum tubes) was a woman, Beverly Strickland (Klein). Her primary duties appear to have been computer programming, which initially required a degree. The digital computers with their capacity for rapid data reduction began to replace the hand calculations. During the early years of the digital computers, most engineers relied on computer programmers to write the data reduction programs required to calculate the desired parameters. Two women programmers, Constance Eaton (Harney) and Elsie McGowan, were hired during this time.

Onboard magnetic tape recording systems began to be used in the late 1960s. The oscillograph film recording systems were soon replaced by these onboard magnetic tape recording systems.[‡] The work done by the women computers was no longer needed and their jobs eventually changed to running the computer programs written by other people. Four of the women computers moved to other jobs. Mary Little, who had a math degree, became chief of the programming and data processing branch. Three of the

[†] The co-op program for engineering students is, as the name would suggest, a cooperative work-study program between the NACA or (later) NASA and different universities. Engineering students alternate between work periods at a NASA (NACA until October 1958) site and their course work at the university.

[††] The X-3, flight tested from 1954 to 1956, had a low-aspect-ratio, thin wing.

[†††] Some women stayed only a few months. I did not try to identify them.

[‡] However, the oscillographs were still used for years on some individual experiments.

† Katharine was sometimes called Kay and Roxanah sometimes called Roxie, especially by friends near their age and time at Dryden. I usually called them by their full names, Katharine and Roxanah, however.

†† The primary test involved an anti-misting fuel additive that was supposed to eliminate rapid burning following an airplane crash. The Boeing 720 was flown by remote control during the controlled impact (crash) demonstration flight. The large fireball and burning after the crash demonstrated that the anti-misting fuel was not as effective as had been expected.

††† ERAST is a program for remotely piloted aircraft that tests aircraft intended ultimately to operate at altitudes up to 100,000 feet for environmental sampling missions of a week or more.

former women computers, Roxanah Yancey, Katharine Armistead,† and Betty Scott Love, moved to engineering positions at this time. Roxanah had a math degree, Katharine a degree in education, and Betty did not have a degree. The remaining women computers eventually quit, retired, or were reassigned to other jobs.

Roxanah and Betty had a relatively easy transition to the engineering field; Katharine did not. By relatively easy transition, I mean that they seemed happy with their work and their promotions. Katharine seemed frustrated, had a difficult time getting promoted, and never did reach the same promotion level as Roxanah or Betty. Some of Katharine's difficulties may have been due to the lack of a strong mentor. Toward the end of her career, Katharine was the lead author on a report. Being a lead author was a source of pride for her.

The next change in the hiring and job requirements for women was also related to digital computers. As the digital computers became more powerful, they were used to run the airplane simulators. The early simulators were based on analog systems, and the programs used to drive them were maintained and run by men. The programming function for the analog computers was literally wired by the programmers into the desired configuration. Analog circuit diagrams were used to plan the wiring configuration, which used circuit components such as resistors, capacitors or diodes to obtain the desired response. Examples of desired responses are summing, integrating, and multiplying. However, the programming function for the digital computers operated using lines of code. Initially, these lines of code were entered into the computer by using computer cards. Each computer card (7 3/8 by 3 1/4 inches) had one line of code (maximum 80 characters) that was entered on the card with a keypunch machine. The keyboard for the keypunch was similar to a typewriter keyboard. A digital program contained several hundred to a thousand or more lines of code. As digital computers began to replace the analog systems, women were hired to run and maintain simulation programs. Martha Evans was the first woman hired to work with the simulation programs. Hybrid analog-digital simulations were used for a few years (for example, the X-15-2 simulation). The first all-digital simulation was for the 3/8-scale F-15 Remotely Piloted Research Vehicle (RPRV). Computer simulation programs require much attention to detail and this need provided an opening for women to work in the simulation area. Women were more easily accepted in any engineering position where the chief require-

Table 2. Number of Women In Technical Fields and Airplane Projects from 1960s to December 1995		
Period	Number	Major Aircraft Projects
1960 - 1969	14	Lifting bodies (M2-F2, HL-10), Lunar Landing Research Vehicle (LLRV), X-15, XB-70 Valkyrie (Mach 3 bomber design)
1970 - 1979	17	F-111 Integrated Propulsion Control System (IPCS), F-111 Transonic AirCraft Technology (TACT), F-8 Digital Fly-by-Wire (DFBW), F-8 Supercritical Wing, Highly Maneuverable Aircraft Technology Remotely Piloted Research Vehicle (HiMAT RPRV), KC-135 Winglets, Lifting bodies (M2-F3, HL-10, X-24A, X-24B), 3/8-scale F-15 (RPRV), Shuttle Orbiter approach and landing tests, YF-12 Blackbird (Mach 3+, evolved into SR-71)
1980 - 1989	26	Boeing 720 Controlled Impact Demonstration (CID††), F-111 Mission Adaptive Wing (MAW), F-111 TACT, F-15 Highly Integrated Digital Electronic Controls (HIDEC), F-16 XL Supersonic Laminar Flow Control (SLFC), F-18 High Alpha Research Vehicle (HARV), HiMat RPRV, X-29 (forward swept wing)
1990 - 1993	26	CV-990 Landing Systems Research Aircraft, F-15 HIDEC, F-16 XL SLFC, F-18 HARV, X-29, SR-71 Blackbird, X-31 Enhanced Fighter Maneuverability program
March 1994	24	CV-990 Landing Systems Research Aircraft, F-15 Advanced Control Technology for Integrated Vehicles (ACTIVE), F-16 XL SLFC, F-18 HARV, F-18 Systems Research Aircraft (SRA), SR-71, X-31
December 1995	21	F-15 ACTIVE, Environmental Research Aircraft and Sensor Technology (ERAST†††) program, F-16 XL SLFC, F-18 HARV, F-18 SRA, SR-71

Figure 18. Airplanes in hanger in late 1966. From front to rear: left side, lifting bodies HL-10, M2-F2, M2-F1; F-4; F-5D; F-104; and DC-3; right side, X-15-1, X-15-3, and X-15-2. (NASA Photo EC66 1461)

ment was attention to detail. The attitude that women were best suited for work that required attention to detail was also found in other scientific fields. An example of this is provided by the following quotation: "Until the second half of this century, male astronomers (with a few exceptions) generally assumed that their female colleagues were better at tedious data inspection than at creative thinking."[18]

Women in Technical Areas from 1960s to Present

The women computers of the late 1940s and early 1950s worked closely with the engineers, almost as though they were junior engineers. By the early 1960s, this working relationship, with four exceptions, no longer existed. These four woman (three retired in 1973, one in 1979) are included in Table 2 in the numbers of women[†] from 1960 to December 1995. The 24 women for March 1994 represent 13% of the engineering work force and the 21 women for December 1995 represent 12%. The major aircraft projects (alphabetical listing) are also included in table 2.

Some of the airplanes mentioned in Table 2 are seen in the group airplane photographs of Figures 18 to 20. Figure 18 shows the airplanes in the hangar being worked on by the aircraft maintenance crews in late 1966. This figure, like Figure

15, shows no women working on the planes.

In the 1970s, women began working on the aircraft maintenance crews (usually only one or two women). Presently three women (two, mechanics; one in avionics) work on these crews. In general, the women had great difficulty fitting in and until the mid- to late 1980s, none continued to work on the crews. (One changed to a job she liked better, one went to college, but most left because of a difficult working environment.) One obvious difficulty for these women was working in a traditional male job. Another was that while most men develop their mechanical skills at an early age, many women do not. This means that using even simple tools, such as pliers or a screwdriver, is not second nature to many women. Those women with limited mechanical skills had an especially difficult time. Most women began working on the aircraft maintenance crews because the upward mobility programs[††] of the late 1970s gave them an opportunity to move from lower paying clerical jobs to higher paying aircraft maintenance crew jobs.

Appendix D shows the type of work and the number of women in each type of work. Of the 24 women working in the technical field in March 1994, 13 were in the engineering disciplines, 3 were in

[†] From 1963 to the present, I have personal knowledge of the women who worked in technical fields at Dryden. Discussions with coworkers ensured I hadn't forgotten anyone. I arrived at dates by asking the women who were still here when those who had left came to Dryden, from my own and my coworkers memories about when women were at Dryden, and from Frank William (Bill) Burcham's collection of Dryden telephone books from 1966 to the present.

[††] The purpose of the upward mobility programs was to provide lower paid employees with positions that had career development opportunities into higher paying jobs. The applicants did not have to meet standard requirements for the job because they were to receive on-the-job training.

Figure 19. Airplanes on ramp, 1988. From front to back and left to right: X-29, AD-1, PA-30, HiMAT, F-104, F-8 DFBW, F-16 AFTI, T-38, F-18, F-18, F-111 MAW, F-15, Rotor Systems Research Aircraft, B-52, Jetstar and 747 shuttle carrier aircraft. (NASA Photo EC88 0042-1)

airplane simulation, 4 were in program management (1 was the acting deputy chief for the division responsible for program management and 1 was also a flight test engineer on the SR-71 crew), 3 were in nondisciplinary management, and 1 was deputy chief of the division responsible for computer systems, flight control rooms, and information networks. By December 1995, the numbers of women

Figure 20. Airplanes on ramp, 1990. Front to back and left to right: F-18 HARV, X-29, F-15, F-16 XL SLFC, 3 F-18 support aircraft, T-38, F-104, B-52, Pegasus, SR-71 and 747 shuttle carrier aircraft. (NASA Photo EC90 280-1)

working in the technical field had decreased to 21. The deputy chief of the division responsible for computer systems, flight control rooms, and information networks, Connie Harney, had retired and the acting deputy chief for program management had returned to her former position. Of the 21 women working in the technical field in December 1995, 11 were in the engineering disciplines, 1 was in airplane simulation, 3 were in program management (1, Marta Bohn-Meyer, continues as a flight test engineer on the SR-71 crew), and 6 were in nondisciplinary management.

Appendix C contains the names of the women who worked at NASA Dryden from 1960 to December 1995. It was difficult to determine the period when women had worked at Dryden. What added to the problem for the women from 1946 to 1954 was that women often change their last name after marriage. Sometimes, what seemed to be two different women were actually the same person. From 1960 on, the name changes were not a problem for me. The name changes could certainly be confusing for somebody who did not personally know most of these women. Because of this, I have included the names found as authors or in documents[†] that included the women working at Dryden. As a point of interest, six of the women presently working at Dryden in the technical field were in its co-op program. Throughout the years, quite a few women have been in the co-op program, but I do not know the number. Some of the co-ops, both women and men, were authors or co-authors on reports. Being an author depended on several factors, including the policy at that time about co-ops being authors and the availability of a suitable project during the co-op period. The only women co-ops included in Appendix C are those who returned to work as engineers. An exception to this is the women co-ops who were authors but who did not return as engineers. These women are included in a footnote to Appendix C.

[†] These documents included the 1954 Air Force yearbook for Edwards, old Dryden telephone directories, and the Dryden in-house newspaper, the *X-Press*.

Notes

[1] The number of employees at Muroc from September 1946 to the end of 1946 is not easily determined. The edition of the in-house newsletter, the *X-PRESS* (as the *X-Press* was then designated), published for the 10th Anniversary of the first flight to exceed the speed of sound, indicates that 13 persons arrived at Muroc on 30 September 1946. However, an anonymous, undated chronology whose last entry was was January 1954 states that the group started with five men on 30 September 1946 and that the first two women employees arrived in December 1946. To further add to the confusion, the *X-PRESS* for the 25th anniversary of the first flight to exceed the speed of sound states that the X-1 was shipped to Muroc accompanied by 14 employees and shows a photograph of 14 employees. (The photograph's date was not given in the title but was given as late 1946 in a Dryden historical photograph display. The original negative is not in the Dryden negative files.) The title for the photograph says that 8 (including the 2 women) of the original 14 Muroc employees are in the photograph. The amount of travel between Muroc and Langley during this period makes it difficult to determine who and how many persons were at Muroc at any given time, but Richard P. Hallion, *On the Frontier: Flight Research at Dryden, 1946-1981* (Washington, D.C.: NASA SP-4303, 1984), p. 9, accepts the facts stated in the anonymous chronology, that the first 13 employees arrived in three separate increments between 30 September 1946 and December of that year.

[2] More discussion of the flight tests of these two series of aircraft is found in Hallion, *On the Frontier,* pp. 6-85 and 285-314, and in Richard P. Hallion, *Supersonic Flight: Breaking the Sound Barrier, The Story of the Bell X-1 and Douglas D-558* (New York: The Macmillan Company, 1972).

[3] The "XS" became "X" after June 11, 1948, as a result of a change in Air Force designation policy. The four aircraft series, XS-1, XS-2, XS-3, and XS-4, affected by this change became X-1, X-2, X-3, and X-4 after this date. See Hallion, *On the Frontier,* pp. 30-31. For the definition for the acronym "XS," see Hallion, *Supersonic Flight,* p. 41.

[4] Hallion, *On the Frontier.*

[5] The original team of people were sent to Muroc to participate in the XS-1 and D-558 research programs. As time passed, it became apparent that these research programs would last a long time. In addition, other programs were starting and more programs were being considered. Then, on 2 September 1947, Hugh Latimer Dryden became the NACA's director of research. Among his first actions was a directive that made the NACA Muroc unit a permanent facility on 7 September 1947, known as the NACA Muroc Flight Test Unit and managed by the Langley Memorial Aeronautical Laboratory. See Hallion, *On the Frontier,* p. 14.

[6] See Hallion, *On the Frontier,* p. 273.

[7] Hallion, *On the Frontier,* p. 23. He credited the comment about the stage line to an interview with Katharine (Kay) H. Armistead. Katharine (originally from Langley) was one of the people who had concerns about making her career at Muroc. She returned to the Langley area for approximately two years and then came back to Muroc. She stayed the second time until her retirement, whereupon she returned to the Langley area to be near her family.

[8] See George W. Gray, *Frontiers of Flight: The Story of NACA Research* (New York: Alfred A. Knopf, 1948), pp. 57-60.

[9] See Hallion, *On the Frontier,* p. 23.

[10] Recollections of Beverly Cothren, Harriet Smith and Betty Love on 13 June 1996. An interesting aspect of the woman computer jobs concerns a man, Terry Larson, who graduated from a California college in Los Angeles and was looking for a job in the early 1950s. His uncle who worked for the state employment office knew that a position was posted for a computer at Muroc. Terry (holding a degree in meteorology with a minor in mathematics) applied. His application was accepted but not for the computer group. He was placed in an engineering job. (Recollections of Terry Larson on 14 June 1996.)

[11] Interview, author with Walt Williams, 17 September 1993. The shortest stay I heard about concerned an engineer from an area with many trees and much grass (east or mid-west) who had just graduated from college. This story was usually told to new engineers from green areas (such as Iowa) when they commented about how different the desert was from home. Nobody ever remembered his name and they weren't sure of the date but it was sometime in the 1950s. The young man reported to work in the morning, was given a tour and shown where he would be sitting. By noon, he had gone to personnel, quit his job and was on his way home.

[12] See Hallion, *On the Frontier*, p. 11. Hallion attributed this quotation to an interview with Katherine Armistead.

[13] See M. D. Keller, "A History of the Langley Research Center, 1917-1947" (Ann Arbor, Michigan: University Microfilms, 1968), p. 253. For another discussion of women at Langley during the war, see James R. Hansen, *Engineer in Charge: A History of the Langley Aeronautical Laboratory, 1917-1958* (Washington, D.C.: NASA SP-4303, 1984), pp. 262-265.

[14] See Marston Muses, "WW II Propels Women into Engineering," *The College of Engineering Alumni News*, Fall 1993, Iowa State University, p. 3.

[15] See Hallion, *On the Frontier*, pp. 262-265.

[16] Joan M. Childs, *Flight Measurements of the Stability Characteristics of the Bell X-5 Research Airplane in Sideslips at 59° Sweepback* (Washington, D.C.: NACA RM L52K13b, 1953).

[17] According to the recollections of Mary Little Kuhl on 29 October 1992.

[18] Marcia Bartusiak, "Focal Point: Shifting the gender spotlight," *Sky & Telescope* (May 1994): 6-7.

Appendixes

† Carmelita (Lita) was head of the editorial office when I started working at Dryden in 1963. Helen, who established the office in 1952, was probably the head of it until she left in 1960.

†† The 15-year pin article also mentioned a stag dinner party held to honor the three men. The article states that the presentation of these pins raised the total of 15-year pin holders to 9. The only woman in the 9 was Helen Foley. It seems too bad that Helen would have been excluded from the party simply because of her gender.

The *X-PRESS* began as a publication for the employees of the NACA High-Speed Flight Station (HSFS). A copy (Volume 2, Issue 3) that was published May 17, 1957, still exists. The volume number indicates that the *X-PRESS* was first published in 1956. Interpreting the issue number is a little confusing because of the publishing comment in the credit block. In the credit block is the statement "Published bi-weekly for employees of NACA High-Speed Flight Station." Possibly at this time, the *X-PRESS* was just beginning to be a regular publication. Other information in this credit block is: Managing Editor, Helen Foley; Editor, Carmelita Holleman; Repro-duction, Walter McIver and Jack Corbin; and Photographers, Robert Rhine and John Bostain.

Helen Foley was a former woman computer who established the library and editorial office and Carmelita Holleman† worked in the editorial office. For several years, the editorial office was responsible for publishing the *X-PRESS*. Sometime in the late 1950s or early 1960s, the Public Affairs Office began assuming responsibil-ity for the publishing. The publishing cycle has varied from every two weeks to monthly, with some hiatuses.

The content has also changed over the years. The 17 May 1957 edition contained announcements and articles of local interest such as Armed Forces Day at Edwards, a Red Cross drive, new hires, safety comments, a reminder to vote in the local school board election, most-sick-leave race, flight lines (comments about births, marriages, a talk given in Lancaster, and reserve unit duty), and a write-up about three men receiving 15-year service pins.†† The present *X-PRESS* contains some articles and announcements similar to these, but it also contains more general interest articles such as NASA news from elsewhere and brief summaries of recent flight activities.

The *X-PRESS* shown was an extra edition published for the 10th anniversary of the first flight to exceed the speed of sound (Mach 1). This *X-PRESS* includes a brief background of the X-1 program, articles by Walter C. Williams (Chief, High Speed Flight Station) and De E. Beeler (Chief, Research Division), a *Los Angles Times* announcement about breaking the sound barrier, some photographs from the late 1940s and short biographies of 10 people. These were people who had started at Muroc in 1946 or 1947 (some were involved with the XS-1 program) and who were still working at HSFS in October 1957. All 14 pages of the extra edition are shown below. Note that they contain some errors and anachronisms, such as referring to the Army Air Forces as the Air Force before the latter was officially so desig-nated in September 1947, but the informa-tion contained in this document is largely correct and provides an interesting reflec-tion of people's memories 10 years after the event.

10TH ANNIVERSARY—SUPERSONIC FLIGHT

X-PRESS

| Extra Edition | NACA HSFS, Edwards, California | October 14, 1957 |

THE X-1 STORY

IN THE DISPLAY IN THE LOBBY OF THE NACA HIGH-SPEED FLIGHT STATION ARE MODELS OF SOME OF THE COUNTRY'S MOST NOTABLE RESEARCH AIRPLANES. THERE IS AN XF-92A, X-3, X-4, X-2, X-5, D-558, PHASE I AND PHASE II, AND THE MOST FAMOUS OF THEM ALL, THE X-1. TEN YEARS AGO - ON OCTOBER 14, 1947 - THE X-1-1 BECAME THE FIRST AIRPLANE TO PIERCE THE SONIC BARRIER, A FEAT DUPLICATED SHORTLY AFTER BY THE X-1-2. TODAY THE X-1-1 HOLDS AN HONORED SPOT IN THE SMITHSONIAN INSTITUTION, AND X-1-2 HAS BEEN MODIFIED AND RE- NAMED THE X-1E. STILL IN ACTIVE STATUS ON THE HSFS FLIGHT LINE ARE THE X-1B AND THE X-1E.

IN THESE TEN YEARS THE NAME OF THE NACA INSTALLATION AT MUROC HAS BEEN CHANGED FROM THE ORIGINAL MUROC FLIGHT TEST UNIT TO THE PRESENT HIGH- SPEED FLIGHT STATION; ITS PERSONNEL HAS INCREASED FROM 27 TO 300; AND, IN 1954, ITS FACILITY EXPANDED FROM 2 ROOMS AND HANGAR SPACE SHARED WITH THE AIR FORCE IN 1946 TO A MODERN TWO-STORY BUILDING FLANKED ON EITHER SIDE BY SPACIOUS HANGARS.

THE XS-1 PROJECT

In 1944 contracts were let for construction of the first two research airplanes. Bell Aircraft Corp. began design of the X-1 (originally known as Project MX653 and later as XS-1) under Air Force sponsorship, and the Douglas Aircraft Co. about the same time undertook con- struction of the D-558, sponsored by the Navy. The first of these was to be powered by a rocket motor; the second, by a turbojet engine.

First to reach the flight-test stage was the X-1, of which two originally were constructed. The fuselage lines were adapted from the basic shape of a 0.50 calibre bullet. Straight wings, with thick, tapered aluminum skin, were provided to insure enough structural strength to with- stand the loads expected at the altitudes and speeds programmed. The strength factor was specified at 18g, instead of 12g then required for fighters. One set of wings had a thickness of 10 percent, much less than anything then flying; the second set was only 8 percent thick.

The power plant of the X-1 was a four-barrel rocket engine developed by Reaction Motors, Inc., under Navy contract. Each rocket barrel produced 1,500 pounds of thrust, for a total engine thrust of 6,000 pounds.

In the fall of 1945, before the rocket engine was ready, the airframe of the X-1 was completed. To save time, Bell engineers proposed carrying the airplane aloft in a "mother ship," then releasing it to fly without power. In this way the general airworthiness of the X-1 could be determined before the rocket motor was completed. These tests were conducted early in 1946 at Pinecastle Air Force Base, Florida, and a group from the Langley Laboratory was sent to maintain and operate the 500 pounds of instrumentation carried by the X-1 and to provide technical guidance. The "mother ship" technique has been used since with others of the research-airplane series.

Following the successful glide tests it was decided that, in the interest of maximum safety for the pilot, powered flights should be made in the vicinity of the largest available landing area. The choice was the Air Force installation on the edge of Rogers Dry Lake in the Mojave Desert of California, known then as Muroc and now as Edwards Air Force Base.

After installation of the R. M. I. engine at Bell Aircraft's Niagara Falls plant, the first of two X-1 research airplanes was taken to Edwards early in October 1946. The previous month, 13 engineers, instrument technicians, and technical observers, all from Langley, were designated the NACA Muroc Flight Test Unit. On September 30 they began work at the desert base. The first successful rocket-powered flight was made December 9 by Chalmers H. ("Slick") Goodlin, company test pilot. By June 1947 performance up to a Mach number of 0.8 was fully demonstrated by Bell Aircraft pilots in a series of 21 powered flights.

On June 30, at a meeting at Wright-Patterson Air Force Base the Air Force and NACA agreed to divide responsibilities. Each agency was to use one of the X-1 airplanes in complementary flight programs. The Air Force objective was to exploit the airplane's maximum performance in as few flights as were reasonable, consistent with safety. The NACA program was necessarily more extensive: to acquire the desired detailed information. The NACA group, now permanently assigned at Edwards, was to furnish engineering and instrumentation assistance to the Air Force group, while the air launching of the NACA airplane was to be handled by the Air Force.

The Air Force received its X-1 in August 1947; mechanical difficulties delayed flights of the other model by the NACA until after the first of the year. The historic first supersonic flight was made on October 14, 1947, by then Capt. Charles E. Yeager, USAF. On March 4, 1948, NACA pilot Herbert Hoover became the first civilian to fly faster than sound.

The following quotation from Maj. Gen. Albert Boyd, USAF, himself one of the first to fly supersonically, is given as a summation of the effectiveness of the cooperative program:

"The combination of talents served two purposes. First, the accelerated USAF program permitted a rapid exploration of the capabilities of the X-1 to the highest speed attained; and, secondly, the detailed NACA program provided the comprehensive data needed to develop complete envelopes of aircraft performance which might reveal unsatisfactory flight characteristics at some intermediate point. When considered separately, each program was a notable contribution to flight research, however, when combined, the results stand as a monumental tribute to both the USAF and NACA since the sonic barrier monster was not only completely licked, but a blow-by-blow account of its defeat was recorded for future use.

"The end results of high-speed flight-research programs conducted jointly made available to aircraft designers, for the first time in the history of flight testing, sorely needed information which served a dual purpose. The rapid but sketchy USAF portion of the program supplied answers which went toward determining the military applicability of a research aircraft, whereas the lengthy but detailed NACA program confirmed or refuted wind-tunnel data and at the same time provided information which would permit aircraft designers to avoid dangerous flight characteristics in future military and civilian aircraft of a more advanced design."

THE BACKGROUND
by Walter C. Williams

In order to describe the events leading up to the first supersonic flight in the X-1 by then Air Force Capt. Charles E. Yeager, perhaps it is most important to give the tempo, or mood, of the time.

In this day of Russian satellites, Inter-Continental Ballistic Missiles, bombers and fighters that fly at Mach numbers of 2 or better, jet transports that will carry over 100 people at speeds higher than had been explored at the time of the X-1 flight, it is difficult even for those directly concerned to picture the state of the art as it was then. Up to the inception of the research airplane program, flying as far as we knew had been limited to Mach numbers of 0.8 on a reasonably consistent and safe basis, with a few excursions above 0.8 which in most cases led to serious difficulties of one sort or another--control, buffeting, even loss of the airplane. This, then, was the field we were setting out to explore.

During the acceptance tests of the X-1, the speed was limited to 0.8 Mach number, a limitation set because it was felt that no manufacturer should be forced to guarantee satisfactory characteristics in the relatively unexplored area above 0.8. During the 20 acceptance test flights, a Mach number of 0.8, or perhaps a little better, was reached. The rocket engine system was proved to be a reasonable power plant. It would be well to point out here that our NACA group, along with the Air Force Flight Test group and the manufacturer, was in many ways a very lonely group and was alone in its belief that this project would succeed. I do not wish to imply that we did not have the proper backing. Top management of all concerned gave their wholehearted support to the program; however, at the contemporary level and intermediate supervisory level there were many dismal predictions, such as:

"The program will fold right after the first powered flight as soon as the airplane blows up."

"The drag is too high, you can't even get the speeds."

"From what we know, the airplane will come completely apart a little above 0.9 Mach number."

These and other similar comments were common. But, it might be said, like the bumble bee, we went ahead. In addition to these known fears and comments, England, who had been attempting such testing, had lost the DH-108 in transonic flight, killing the pilot. This led the British to adopt a policy of model testing and possibly remote guidance for the airplanes before they would ever attempt manned supersonic flight. This, without question, set their effort back an unmeasured number of years. These things were all hanging heavy over our heads.

We were enthusiastic, there is little question. The Air Force group--Yeager, Ridley--were very, very enthusiastic. We were just beginning to know each other, just beginning to work together. There had to be a balance between complete enthusiasm and the hard, cold facts. We knew and felt that if this program should fail the whole research airplane program would fail, the whole aeronautical effort would be set back. So, our problem became one of maintaining the necessary balance between enthusiasm and eagerness to get the job completed with a scientific approach that would assure success of the program. This was accomplished.

To say that we went ahead completely on our own would be foolish. We had some information-- acceptance tests showed that low-speed wind-tunnel tests gave an accurate prediction of the behavior characteristics of the airplane. We had some transonic tunnel data up to about 0.85 Mach number that showed things would be reasonably satisfactory. We also had data from the then newly developed wing-flow method, where models were placed in the high-speed flow over a subsonic airplane's wing. These data, however, ended at 0.93 Mach number with various pertinent quantities showing abrupt changes for limits. With this information on hand, and knowing the results of acceptance tests, the joint Air Force-NACA program was started.

As has been pointed out, there were two airplanes involved: the Air Force airplane to exploit the speed potential of the airplane in as short a time as consistent with safety, and the NACA program to provide the detailed information. Actually, an exploratory program, as we have learned, is the first phase in testing of any airplane. The Air Force airplane was ready for flight first, and so began the systematic step-by-step approach to the problem of flying at speeds faster than anyone had flown before, or, to be "corny", thus began the conquest of the sound barrier. Small incremental increases in Mach number were made, making pull-ups at the maximum Mach number to aid in predicting what the characteristics might be at somewhat higher Mach numbers in level flight. The stabilizer effectiveness was checked in flying the airplane; runs were made at several stabilizer settings; actual pull-ups were made using the stabilizer. In the second flight a Mach number of 0.89 was successfully reached in powered flight, after which five or six maneuvering flights were conducted around a Mach number of 0.90 to evaluate trends in elevator and stabilizer effectiveness, wing and balancing horizontal-tail loads, and buffeting. On the eighth flight (October 10, 1947) an indicated Mach number of 0.94 was reached in flight; however, after the flight indicators were corrected for the influence of the airplane's pressure field it was found that the true Mach number was approximately 1. The tabulated data showed 0.997. It wasn't felt that it was a clear-cut case of a sonic flight. It was only a matter of repeating the previous flight, but to a slightly higher speed--this was done on October 14 in flight number nine to a Mach number of 1.06. In this flight, the now typical jump in the airspeed and altitude readings occurred, caused by the bow wave passing over the static-pressure holes. There was then little doubt that highly publicized and feared "sonic barrier" had been breached.   -3-

MUROC IN 1947...a land of plentiful sunshine, warm dry air, the wide open spaces with unlim-
ited visibility and ceiling conditions. MUROC IN 1947...a wind-swept, flat desert area with winds
reaching 50 mph creating dust and sandstorms that reduced both visibility and ceiling conditions
to 400 feet. An area capable of producing temperatures from 5°F to 115°F. MUROC IN 1947...man-
built structures that provided a bare minimum in living comfort by any standards of the day.

Add to this environment, a research aircraft designed with the best aeronautical knowledge of
the day for achieving what man had never done — flight at sonic speed. Add, also, a group with
enough faith, conviction, and pioneering spirit to undertake the detailed planning and execution
of a program to demonstrate the feasibility of attaining sonic flight. These were the ingredients
that set the stage for the period of flight demonstration and the actual flight program at Muroc.

It may be that the pioneering spirit required for coping with the living and working conditions at Muroc had much to do with developing the dedicated group that existed there at the time
of the X-1 flight. It is a certainty that the same pioneering spirit that originally inspired the
individual to want to be a part of the X-1 project was a necessary prerequisite to enable him to
continue to tolerate living in housing facilities equivalent to high-type stables; the ever present
uncertainty of the official status of the group at Muroc even to use such facilities; working in
limited areas and improvising facilities to provide the necessary airplane and instrumentation
equipment for conducting flight tests; working long, irregular hours on their own to accelerate
the project. All this was a part of life at Muroc.

The initial reward for the weary Muroc group came on that October 13, 1947, when they first
realized that a successful flight through the questionable transonic speed regions had been accomplished. Now it was only necessary to extend the flight speed slightly to record an unquestionable
sonic speed.

So, it is, even with all the inconveniences and uncertainties of existence at Muroc in 1947,
that all those dedicated to the X-1 project look back today on their life at Muroc as a good one,
and, as a result of the success of the project, an immeasurably rewarding one.

PERSONNEL DIRECTLY CONNECTED WITH THE XS-1 FLIGHT PROGRAM ON OCTOBER 14, 1947

Of the 27 employees at the Muroc Flight Test Unit in October 1947, 19 were specifically assign-
ed to the XS-1 project. They were: Walter Williams, De Beeler, Joseph Vensel, Gerald Truszynski,
Clyde Bailey, Roxanah Yancey, Charles Hamilton, Harold Goodman, John Gardner, Milton McLaughlin,
Frank Hughes, LeRoy Proctor, Jr., Arthur Vernon, Elmer Bigg, Phyllis Actis, Dorothy Hughes, John
Mayer, and William Beedle and John Russell, both assigned from the Air Force.

PRESENT HSFS EMPLOYEES DIRECTLY CONNECTED WITH THE XS-1 FLIGHT PROGRAM ON OCTOBER 14, 1947

R. Yancey, D. Beeler, J. Russell, J. Vensel, W. Williams, C. Hamilton, G. Truszynski, C. Bailey.

-4-

Los Angeles Times

VOL. LXVII   *** A   MONDAY MORNING, DECEMBER 22, 1947   DAILY, FIVE CENTS

U.S. MYSTERY PLANE TOPS SPEED OF SOUND

Test Pilots Pierce Dread Barrier at 70,000 Feet Altitude Above Desert

BY MARVIN MILES

Three Americans have pierced the wall of sound!

The dread barrier to supersonic flight was first conquered at Muroc Air Base early last month when Capt. Charles Yaeger, Air Force pilot, hurtled the XS-1 rocket plane through the wall at approximately 70,000 feet, The Times learned from reliable sources.

5

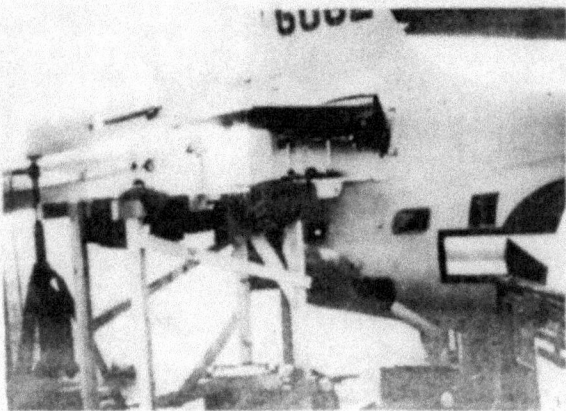

35

7

Top (left to right) - FHA Dormitory "C", Base Post Office Center - Aerial view of Base
Bottom - Dot Clift, Base hospital; Roxie Yancey, Women's Dorm; Dot Clift, Officers Club pool

8

Top (left to right) - WILLOW SPRINGS pool, tavern, Hamilton home, Pony Express relay station
Center - Muroc school Bottom - Bailey home (summer and winter) in Mojave Naval Housing

PERSONNEL OF MUROC FLIGHT TEST UNIT ON OCTOBER 14, 1957

On October 14, 1947, the Muroc Flight Test Unit, headed by Walter C. Williams, was staffed by 25 NACA'ers and 2 Air Force civilian employees.

In Research Engineering, with De E. Beeler as head, were engineers Eugene D. Beckwith, Hubert M. Drake, Harold R. Goodman, Milton D. McLaughlin, and John P. Mayer (temporarily assigned from Langley). Computers under the direction of Roxanah B. Yancey were Phyllis Rogers Actis and Dorothy Clift Hughes.

Joseph R. Vensel was in charge of the Operations staff, composed of Howard C. Lilly and Herbert Hoover (pilots), Clyde G. Bailey, Elmer W. Bigg, Donald E. Borchers, John J. Gardner, Charles M. Hamilton, Harold J. Nemecek, Richard E. Payne, and John W. Russell (assigned from the Air Force).

The Instrumentation division, under the supervision of Gerald M. Truszynski, was made up of Frank M. Hughes, George Minalga, LeRoy Proctor, Jr., Arthur W. Vernon, and William C. Beedle (assigned from the Air Force).

Naomi C. Wimmer handled the secretarial duties for the Unit.

PRESENT HSFS EMPLOYEES WHO WERE ASSIGNED TO MUROC FLIGHT TEST UNIT IN OCTOBER 1947

Seated (left to right) - Gerald M. Truszynski, Chief, Instrumentation; Joseph R. Vensel, Chief, Operations; Walter C. Williams, Chief of the Station; Roxanah B. Yancey, Supervisory Mathematician. Standing - Charles M. Hamilton, Assistant Superintendent, Flight Maintenance; Clyde G. Bailey, Superintendent, Flight Maintenance; Hubert M. Drake, Assistant Chief, Research; John W. Russell, Rocket Group Leader; De E. Beeler, Chief, Research; Richard E. Payne, Crew Chief.

10

39

PERSONALITIES

WALTER C. WILLIAMS

As assistant head of the Langley Flight Research Division stability and control section, Walt's direct contact with the XS-1 program began shortly after its initiation in 1945, when he worked with Milt Davidson (Langley) to coordinate test requirements among Bell, the Air Force, and NACA. From January to March of 1946, Walt acted as NACA project engineer during preliminary glide flights of the XS-1 then being made at Pinecastle AAB (Rogers Dry Lake was flooded). When, as a result of these tests, it was determined that an air launch operation was feasible, and that all further testing should be performed at Muroc, Walt was transferred to the desert site in September 1946. He was joined by his wife, Helen, and four-year old son, Charles, the following month, after an apartment was found in Palmdale.

Three months later the Williams' moved to the Naval Housing project in Mojave, and in 1949 moved to 5000 Area on the Base. In 1951 they purchased a home in Lancaster, in which they are residing with Charles Manning, now 15, Howard Lee, 9, and Elizabeth Anne, 5.

DE E. BEELER

De became associated with the research airplane program in 1945 in the Langley Aircraft Loads Division and was assigned to Muroc in January 1947 as X-1 project engineer in charge of the aircraft loads program.

After living in BOQ "D" Barracks at Muroc about six months, he moved with John Mayer of Langley to a ranch apartment on Rosamond Dry Lake (with trees, flowers, grass, and two lakes). From Rosamond he returned to Muroc and BOQ "B", where he lived with HSFS pilot Howard Lilly. He later moved to the NACA Men's Dorm and resided there until 1952 when he began construction of his present home in Lancaster.

In 1952 De was married to the former Florence Deacon. They have two children--Susan, 4, and De Elroy, II, 8 months.

JOSEPH R. VENSEL

Joe transferred from Lewis Laboratory to Muroc in April 1947 as chief of flight operations for NACA's fledgling Muroc Flight Test Unit. In the days when propellant "leaks" were plaguing the small project group, advice and encouragement were always forthcoming from Joe.

Joe was joined by his wife, Frances, and three children--Dick, now 18, Joan, 13, and Mary Ellen, 12--in August 1947. They resided in the Mojave Naval Housing until October 1948, when they purchased the house in which they now live in Lancaster.

-11-

40

GERALD M. TRUSZYNSKI

Jerry's original association with the XS-1 project began in 1946 during the initial drops of the XS-1 airplane at Pinecastle Army Air Base, Florida, where he was concerned with setting up a ground radar to record the drops. After transfer of the project to Murco in 1946, he again caught up with it in March 1947 as the instrumentation project engineer. After living for some time at Mojave Naval Housing, he and his wife, Helen, moved to Lancaster in 1949, where they now reside. They have two children--Joan Marie, 2 1/2, and Carl Gerald, 10 months.

CLYDE G. BAILEY

Clyde first arrived at Muroc in January 1947 on one year's temporary duty. His wife, Mildred, and three-year old daughter, Sandra ("Button"), moved to the desert from Virginia in April 1947. Naval Housing in Mojave provided living quarters for the Baileys until June 1950.

As group leader, Clyde's primary duties on the XS-1 project were with mechanical groups from both the NACA and the Air Force.

Clyde, his wife, and three children--Sandra, 13, Heather, 5, and Berkley, 8 months, now live in Lancaster.

ROXANAH B. YANCEY

For Roxie, the X-1 project was a four-month temporary assignment that has ballooned into a permanent 10-year position.

Upon arriving at Muroc in December 1946, Roxie began at Kerosene Flats (so named because of the heating method) what was to become a 2-year nomadic existence. From Kerosene Flats, she went to housing opened in the hospital area by the Air Force-- then to the Air Force nurses' quarters, made available to Civil Service personnel for a limited time--next, to the "Guest House" for three days--and, for 5 years, to the NACA Women's Dorm.

After a 4-year residence in Wherry Housing, Roxie now lives in Edgemont Acres, a community north of the present Base.

-12-

41

CHARLES M. HAMILTON

"Mac", a former Bell employee, was assigned to the MX-653 Project early in 1945 as crew chief. In February 1946 the airplane was flown to Pinecastle AAB, Florida, under B-29 No. 800, where glide tests were conducted by Jack Wollams, chief test pilot for Bell Aircraft. Here, NACA'ers Walt Williams, Jerry Truszynski, and Norm Hayes joined the project for operation of instrumentation and radar which Mac operated in flight.

After successful glide tests, the airplane was returned to the Bell plant for installation of the rocket powerplant and was redesignated the XS-1. After several successful ground runs, the project was flown to Muroc, arriving on October 21, 1946.

At that time rental housing was almost nonexistent on the desert, but weeks of hunting finally got Mac's family located on the Lahitte Ranch 40 miles west of the Base.

On completion of Bell's flight demonstration program, Mac was employed by NACA on August 12, 1947, and continued as crew chief and flight crew member on further flight test programs.

Mac, his wife, Alice, and children--Grierson, then 9, and Patricia, 8,--later lived at Willow Springs for 3 years during which time their California baby, Mary Alice, was born at Mojave Hospital. In 1950 Mac's family built their present home at Lancaster.

HUBERT M. DRAKE

"Jake's" first visit to Muroc was made during a vacation trip in June 1947. Impressed by the work then being conducted here by NACA, he later readily accepted an offer to transfer from Langley to Muroc as stability and control engineer.

In October 1947, Jake, his wife, Eleanor, and son, David, arrived in Muroc. For 4 years after their arrival, they lived in the Naval Housing in Mojave.

The Drakes with their three children--David, 13, Catherine Rose, 6, and Carol Ann, 3--now live in Lancaster.

JOHN W. RUSSELL

Jack's association with the desert began in 1942, when as a mechanic for Bell Aircraft of Buffalo, New York, he was assigned to the highly secret P-59 jet project at Muroc. With his wife, Ruth, he set up his residence in the (then) "wilderness" of Tenth Street West in Lancaster.

During his second Muroc assignment in 1946 (on the XS-1 project), he, his wife, and son, John Jr., lived in Willow Springs in a settlement made up principally of Bell personnel.

In August 1947, Jack was employed by the Air Force as crew chief on the XS-1 and participated in the airplane's delivery to the Smithsonian Institution. He joined the NACA as an aircraft mechanic on the X-1 project in January 1950.

Jack and his family, which now also includes Jimmy, 9, reside in Rosamond.

-13-

42

RICHARD E. PAYNE

As a "single" aircraft mechanic transferring from Lewis Lab, Cleveland, Dick first began work at Muroc in October 1947, where he shared quarters in Base housing with Howard Lilly. In January 1948, after a trip to Cleveland, he resumed work at Muroc---a married man. He and his bride, Mary, began housekeeping in the Mojave Naval Housing, but shortly after moved to Willow Springs. For three years, prior to the birth of Clyde Richard in 1951, Mary was employed as a computer with the NACA.

The Paynes began construction in 1949 of their present "home on the hill", 3/4 mile north of Rosamond.

PROGRAM AND DINNER COMMEMORATE XS-1 SUPERSONIC FLIGHT

Today, October 14--the tenth anniversary of man's first airplane flight faster than the speed of sound--will be marked at HSFS by a commemorative program and dinner.

The program, to be attended by HSFS employees, is scheduled for 3 p.m. in the Calibration Hangar and will feature talks by Air Force Lt. Col. Charles E. Yeager, who piloted the X-1 on the first supersonic flight; Hartley A. Soulé, Langley Research Airplane Projects Leader; and Chief of the Station Walter C. Williams. The talks will recount various highlights of the X-1 program and pay honor to pilot Yeager and the NACA employees who worked on the preparation and subsequent successful execution of the record-making flight.

Tonight, at 7:30, a dinner at the Antelope Valley Inn in Lancaster will be attended by those closely associated with the X-1's development and first flight through the sonic barrier. Each guest will receive a small plaque, made from the material of the windshield of the original X-1, engraved with an anniversary inscription commemorative of the historical first flight.

X-1-1 IN SMITHSONIAN INSTITUTION

43

Appendix B: Data Reduction and Instrumentation Before Digital Computers

This appendix is divided into four main sections. The first deals with the oscillograph film recorder system; the second, with the procedure used to read the film; the third with tools used in reading the film and producing the final plots; and the fourth is a time history plot and event log for an X-15 aircraft flight.

Oscillograph Film Recorder System

The recorder system shown in Figure B-1 is representative of those used on the X-1 aircraft. The system has an overall length of 13 inches and weighs 12.5 pounds. The system consists of two major parts (fig. B-2). The circular part (5.5-inch

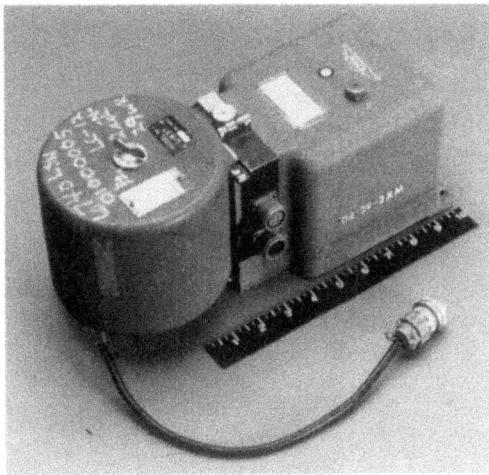

Figure B-1. Photograph of oscillograph film recorder system used to record flow direction. The ruler is in inches. (NASA Photo EC93 42307-1)

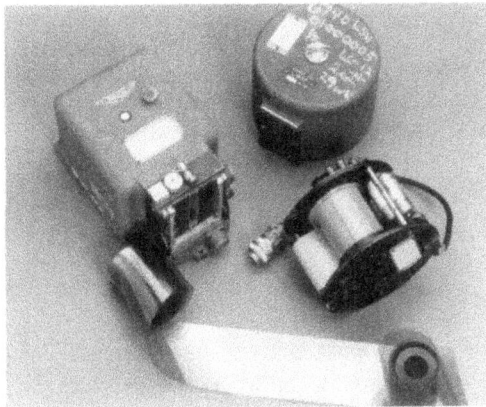

Figure B-2. Oscillograph recorder system shown disassembled with a roll of processed film. (NASA Photo EC93 42307-7)

diameter and a depth of 4.5 inches) contained the film drum. The rectangular part (approximately 5 inches at cube region) contained the "instrument." The recorder system shown in Figures B-1 and B-2 is a flow-direction recorder (note the DR prefix in the legend stenciled on the side of the recorder) that is used to measure the angle of attack and the angle of sideslip of an aircraft. Obviously, the data that were recorded depended on the "instrument." The processed film shown in Figure B-2 as an example is actually from a pressure recorder system.

The outer cases of the instruments were usually limited to a few standard configurations because of space and mounting limitations on the aircraft and because of the need to fit, or interface with, one of the standard film recorder cases. For some experiments, the recorders on the aircraft could be located in a controlled temperature environment compartment. This compartment would minimize temperature effects on the recorder.

Figure B-3 shows the internal components of a temperature-compensated

Figure B-3. Photograph of mirror assembly element (left) and diaphragm element (right) used in a temperature-compensated airspeed recorder. (NASA Photo E3588)

airspeed recorder. The components include two major elements: the rectangular shape contains the mirror system, and the circular shape contains a corrugated diaphragm surrounded by an airtight capsule. The capsule used in the airspeed recorder was a temperature-compensated differential low-pressure capsule. The airspeed recorder used the difference between an impact pressure and a static pressure to measure the aircraft velocity.[†]

tion determines which of the four pivoted mirrors is used. A fixed mirror (reference mirror) is also mounted inside the capsule to provide a reference from which the

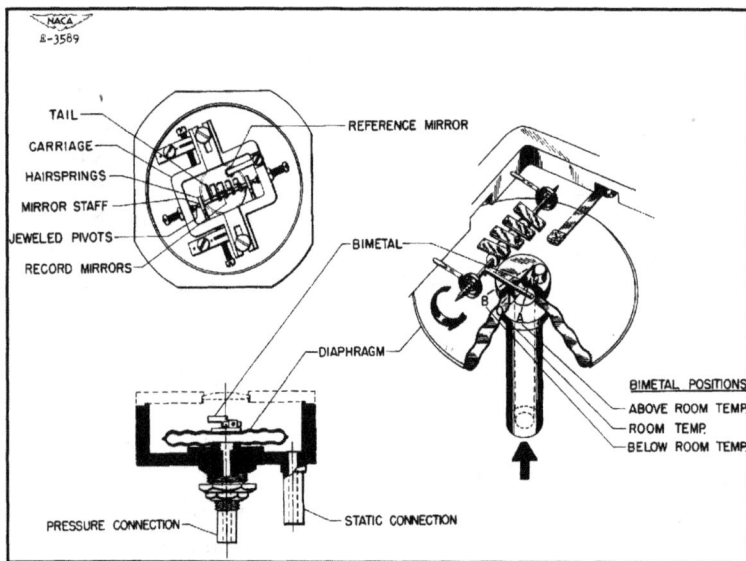

Figure B-4. Schematic showing the different parts of the mirror and diaphragm elements of the temperature-compensated airspeed recorder seen in Figure B-3 (differential pressure measured). (Ilford print)

Figure B-4 shows a schematic identifying the different parts of the airspeed recorder. The pressure connection (connected to impact pressure) is applied to the inside of the diaphragm, and the static connection (connected to static pressure) is applied to the inside of the capsule surrounding the diaphragm. The unsupported end of the diaphragm moves

deflection images are measured. These images are recorded on the film in the film recorder. A bimetal lever arm is located on top of the diaphragm to compensate for temperature changes.

Figure B-5 shows the schematic[††] for the internal components of a temperature-compensated altimeter recorder. This

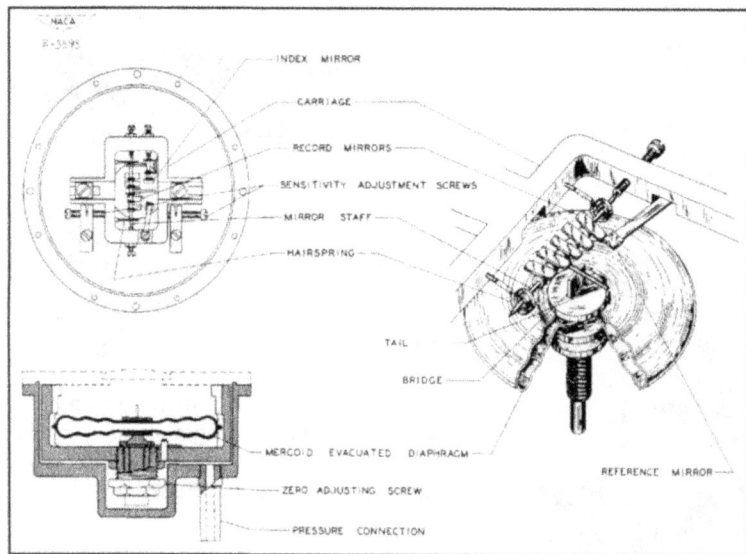

Figure B-5. Schematic showing the different parts of the mirror and diaphragm elements of a temperature-compensated altimeter recorder (absolute pressure measured). (Ilford print)

almost linearly with respect to the difference in pressure applied across it. The deflection of the diaphragm is transmitted to a pivoted mirror that reflects a beam of light through a lens embedded in the capsule front plate. The amount of deflec-

recorder was an absolute pressure recorder. Again, the interior consists of two major elements: the rectangular shape contains the mirror elements, and the circular shape contains an evacuated corrugated diaphragm surrounded by an

[†] The impact and static pressures were obtained using a device called a pitot-static tube (also called a pitot-static head) that is specially designed for airspeed measurements. The static pressure from the pitot-static tube could additionally be used in the operation of an altimeter (which indicated altitude).

[††] The photograph of the mirror assembly (fig. B-3), the schematics (figs. B-4 and B-5), and the descriptions for the schematics were in a notebook compiled earlier (perhaps in the 1960s) by an instrumentation engineer (probably Don Veatch). As people retired, the notebooks (at least two volumes) remained behind. The one used here was in the possession of Wilson E. Vandiver, who had received it from Don Veatch when Don retired. Cleo M. Maxwell, who was one of the X-15 aircraft program instrumentation engineers, was also very helpful in providing information about the oscillograph film recorder systems. (Discussions with Wilson 7 January 1994 and 28 June 1995 and with Cleo 7 January 1994.)

† The width for the 2-inch film actually measured 2.5 inches, and for the 6-inch film, 6.5 inches. I did not have a 12-inch film to measure.

airtight capsule. The pressure connection (connected to the aircraft static pressure) is applied to the inside of the capsule surrounding the diaphragm. One end of the diaphragm is attached to the capsule and the other end is free to move with the variation of absolute pressure. The free end of the diaphragm moves a pivoted

element is constructed from an alloy that has very little change in its modulus of elasticity (stretch or shrinkage) with changes in temperature.

Both of these recorder systems measured only one parameter (one measuring the difference between two

(a) 12-cell pressure manometer; no film drum. Ruler is in inches. (NASA Photo EC94 42599-1)

(b) 24-cell pressure manometer with film drum. Ruler is in inches. (NASA Photo E855)

Figure B-6. Oscillograph recorder systems that measure several parameters.

(c) 24-cell pressure manometer; no film drum. Ruler is in inches. (NASA Photo E856)

mirror that reflects a beam of light through a lens embedded in the capsule front plate. The amount of deflection of the diaphragm determines which of the four pivoted mirrors is used. A fixed mirror (reference mirror) is also mounted inside the capsule to provide a reference from which the deflection images are measured. These images are recorded on the film in the film drum. The diaphragm used in this

pressures and the other, an absolute pressure) and both recorder systems used 2-inch wide film. Some film recorder systems used larger film (for example 6-inches wide† or 12-inches wide) and some recorder systems measured more than one parameter. Figure B-6 shows examples of two pressure manometer systems that measured 12 and 24 parameters. A 36-cell pressure manometer (not shown in the figure) was also used.

The 12-cell manometer [fig. B-6 (a)] was used to measure one absolute pressure and eleven differential pressures. The differential pressures are connected to the manifold tube shown supported by the

47

triangular-shaped brackets. The same pressure source that 'feeds' the manifold also feeds the absolute pressure cell. Therefore, the differential pressures (ranged for plus and minus) would in effect be measured with respect to the pressure for the absolute pressure cell.

The 24-cell manometer [figs. B-6 (b)and (c)] appears to measure only differential pressures. Figure B6 (c) shows the manometer with the film drum removed. A slit, or opening, can be seen between the support rails for the film drum. This glass-covered opening was where the light was reflected from the mirrors to the film.

pressure and the individual pressure.[†] The reference pressure was measured with an absolute pressure instrument similar to the system shown in Figure B-5. In Figure B-6 (a), the P in the P-16-12 notation stands for pressure, the 16 means the instrument was identified as number 16 (each instrument had an identification number), and the 12 means the instrument has 12 cells. The instrument identification number was 6 for the 24-cell pressure manometer [figs. B-6 (b) and (c)].

The systems that measured more than one parameter also had more than one reference trace. The distance between the parameter trace and the reference trace

[†] These manometers operated on a principle similar to that of mechanical and electronic scanning valves. Each cell of the manometer was recorded in sequence. In other words, the pressure difference was recorded for cell 1, then cell 2, then cell 3, and so forth until the final cell was reached. Then the sequence would start over with cell 1. Each trace was displaced horizontally (at least, that was the plan) from the preceding trace and, in addition, there was a small break in the trace between each cell. So once the position for the trace from cell 1 was located, one merely had to number the other traces and keep track of them for the rest of the film. As will be discussed later, labeling the traces was the first of many steps leading to the final data plots.

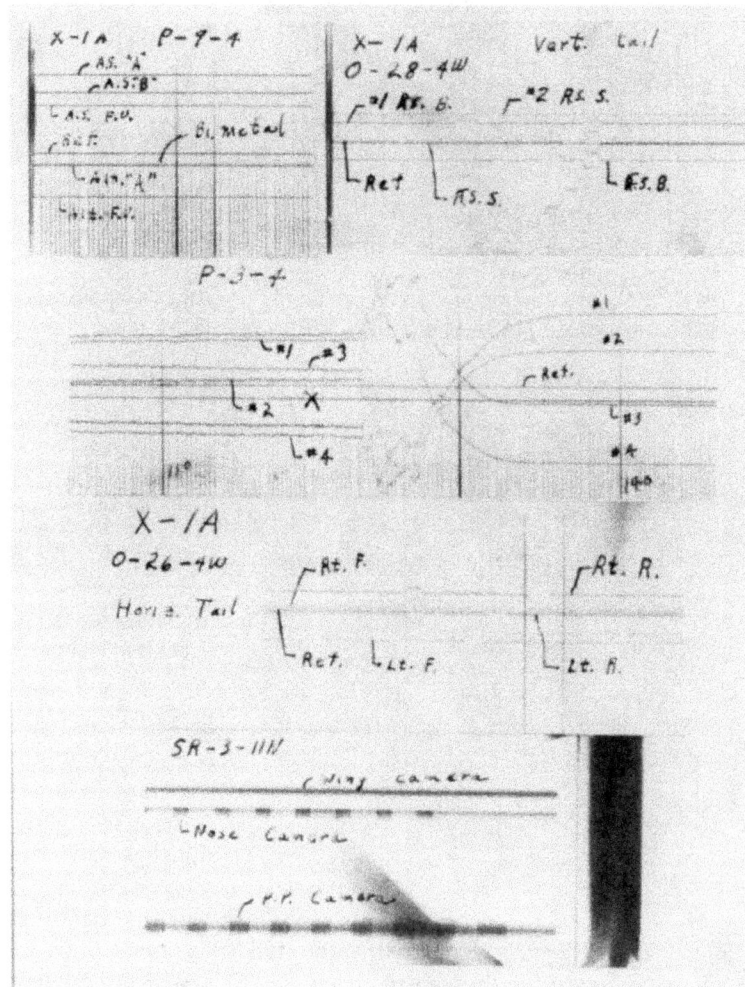

Figure B-7. Film strips used to aid in identification of film traces. (NASA Photo EC93 42307-35)

The multicell systems discussed here worked on the same principal as the single-cell recorders (figs. B-3, B-4 and B-5); but, these systems measured 12 or 24 differential pressures at one time. For the differential cells, the pressure measured was the difference between a reference

was translated into engineering values (for example, pressure, velocity, or angles) by using calibration curves. A system that measured 12 parameters would have 4 reference traces. Each of these 12 parameter traces was associated with a reference trace. For example, the traces for param-

48

† This film showing the
first Mach number jump
was rediscovered by
accident. In the 1970s,
Edwin J. Saltzman
ordered some stored
boxes from the storage
warehouse in the Los
Angeles area. He
discovered the film
when looking through a
box that was sent by
mistake. He believed it
was a film from the first
piloted flight to exceed
the speed of sound. By
reading the film and
analyzing the data, he
confirmed his suspicion.
The film he found is
now in the Smithsonian
Institution's National Air
and Space Museum.

†† Discussions with
Lannie Dean Webb and
Cleo Maxwell on 5 July
1994.

eters 1 through 4 would be associated with
reference trace 1 and the trace for parameter 5 would be associated with reference
trace 2. The film used as an example in
the next section measured two parameters
(impact pressure and static pressure) and
had two reference traces.

Film Reading Procedure

After the films for the flight were
processed, they were laid out and marked
so that each film had the start time (time
equal to zero) on the correct timing mark.
For the X-1 aircraft, this effort involved
film from eight film recorders for typical
flight times of from 10 to 15 minutes. After
the zero time was identified, each film had
the times marked on the film (for example,
every two seconds), and the traces were
identified. Marking the traces with the

The film strip shown in Figure B-8 will
be used to describe the film reading
procedure. This film strip shows the Mach
jump from the first piloted flight to exceed
the speed of sound.† The leading edge
(left edge) of each timer mark is used to
identify a specific time. The time is in
seconds, with the zero time being when
all the film recorders were simultaneously
started by a switch turned on by the pilot.
This switch actually turned on all the
instrumentation, including the film recorders and the single common timing device.†† The single common timer device
generated the time signals used by the
recorders. Each recorder had a "channel,"
or light source, that was triggered by the
master signal from the common timer
device. Thus, the system was designed so
that each recorder made its own timing
marks on the film.

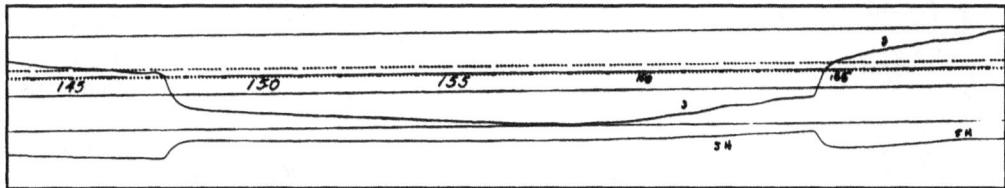

Figure B-8. Film strip from an absolute pressure recorder used to measure an impact pressure
and a pressure static. Time (145, 150, etc.) is in seconds. The numeral 3 means trace is from the
third mirror for the impact pressure trace. The 5H means trace is from the fifth mirror of the static
pressure trace. (NASA Photo E38438) (See figure 11, p. 13, for details)

appropriate labels required skill and
knowledge. Some people would use a roll
of film from an earlier flight to aid in
identifying the traces. Another method was
to use a short strip of the film from an area
where the different traces could be easily
identified, such as when the X-1 aircraft
began its climb after launch. Figure B-7
shows examples of short film strips used
for identifying the traces from X-1A flights.
I was not able to identify all the notations
on the film strips. The notations P-9-4,
0-28-4W, P-3-4, 0-26-4W, and SR-3-11N
identify the recorder (or instrument). The
"A.S." on recorder P-9-4 stands for Air
Speed and "Alt" is altitude. The "Rt. F.",
"Rt. R.", "Lt. F.", and "Lt. R." on the horizontal tail strip (0-26-4W) mean right flap,
right rudder, left flap and left rudder. The
"Ref." identifies the reference trace. The
meanings for the other markings ("A", "B",
"F.U.", "RS.B", "F.S.S.", "R.S.S.", "F.S.B." and
"P.P.") are unknown.

For parameters that needed more than
one mirror, the trace identification required another step. The mirror also had
to be identified. The numeral "3" written
above the impact pressure trace in Figure
B-8 signifies that this trace is caused by a
source light beam reflected off the third
mirror. Similarly, the "5H" written near the
static pressure trace represents the fifth
(and last) mirror for the static pressure
record.

Once the time and the traces were
identified, the film was read. This reading
was done by measuring the deflection, or
distance, from the reference trace to the
respective pressure trace. The distance was
measured normal to the reference trace
with a transparent scale (known as a film
scale) that was calibrated in 0.02-inch
increments. If the traces were very sharp,
an experienced film reader could define
(interpolate) a deflection to the nearest

0.005 inch. When the trace was not sharp, the reading could be made to the nearest 0.01 inch. A light box and a magnifying glass [fig. B-9 (a)] were often used to assist in reading the film. Another method used

heating effects. Reading the film with the telereader, at least before it became more automated, was probably not any faster than using a film scale. I never used a telereader; however, I suspect it was

† Discussions with John W. Smith and Richard E. Klein on 16 September 1993 and Mary Little Kuhl on 19 April 1994.

†† Film in the telereader was read in a dark, isolated room. The darkness improved the contrast for reading the film traces but also earned the room the name "mole hole." (Recollections of Betty Love on 13 June 1996.)

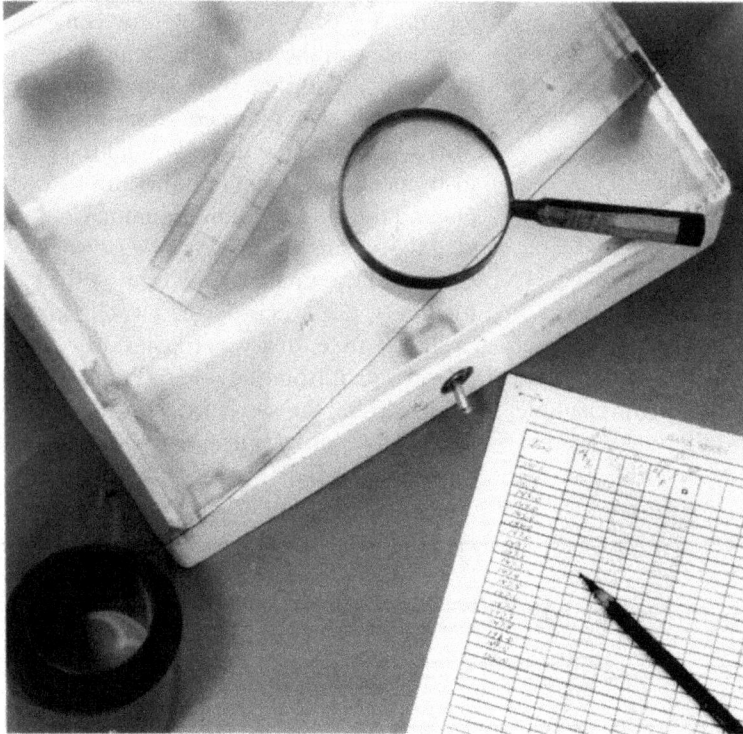

Figure B-9. Two methods used to read film.

Figure B-9 (a) (left). Film shown on a lightbox. The lightbox and magnifying glass were sometimes used to aid in reading the film with a film scale (lying on lightbox). The values read from the film were written on the data sheet. (NASA Photo EC93 42307-6)

Figure B-9 (b) (below). Delores Sutphin demonstrating the use of a telereader machine to read film. No film was being read for this demonstration. (NASA Photo E1006)

to read film, beginning in 1953, involved a telereader machine. Figure B-9 (b) shows a telereader being demonstrated by Delores Sutphin. The technique was to set a zero then move the crosshairs to the data point to be read.† A foot pedal, visible under her right foot, was used to "read" the numbers. Originally, a second person would record the numbers from dials located to the right of Ms. Sutphin. Sometime later, the numbers were printed on a typewriter connected to the telereader. The typewriter seen in this photograph was not connected to the telereader. In the 1960s, the recording procedure was more automated. A typewriter and a card-punch machine were connected to the telereader. When the foot pedal was pressed, the numbers were printed by the typewriter and computer cards were punched. One problem with the telereader concerned the film. Often the film was copied to photosensitive paper. The photosensitive paper would change size with changes in temperature. Because the light source in the telereader heated the photosensitive paper, the readings would have to be adjusted for

slower and that placing the crosshairs required much patience, but at least some thought it was more fun using the telereader to read film.††

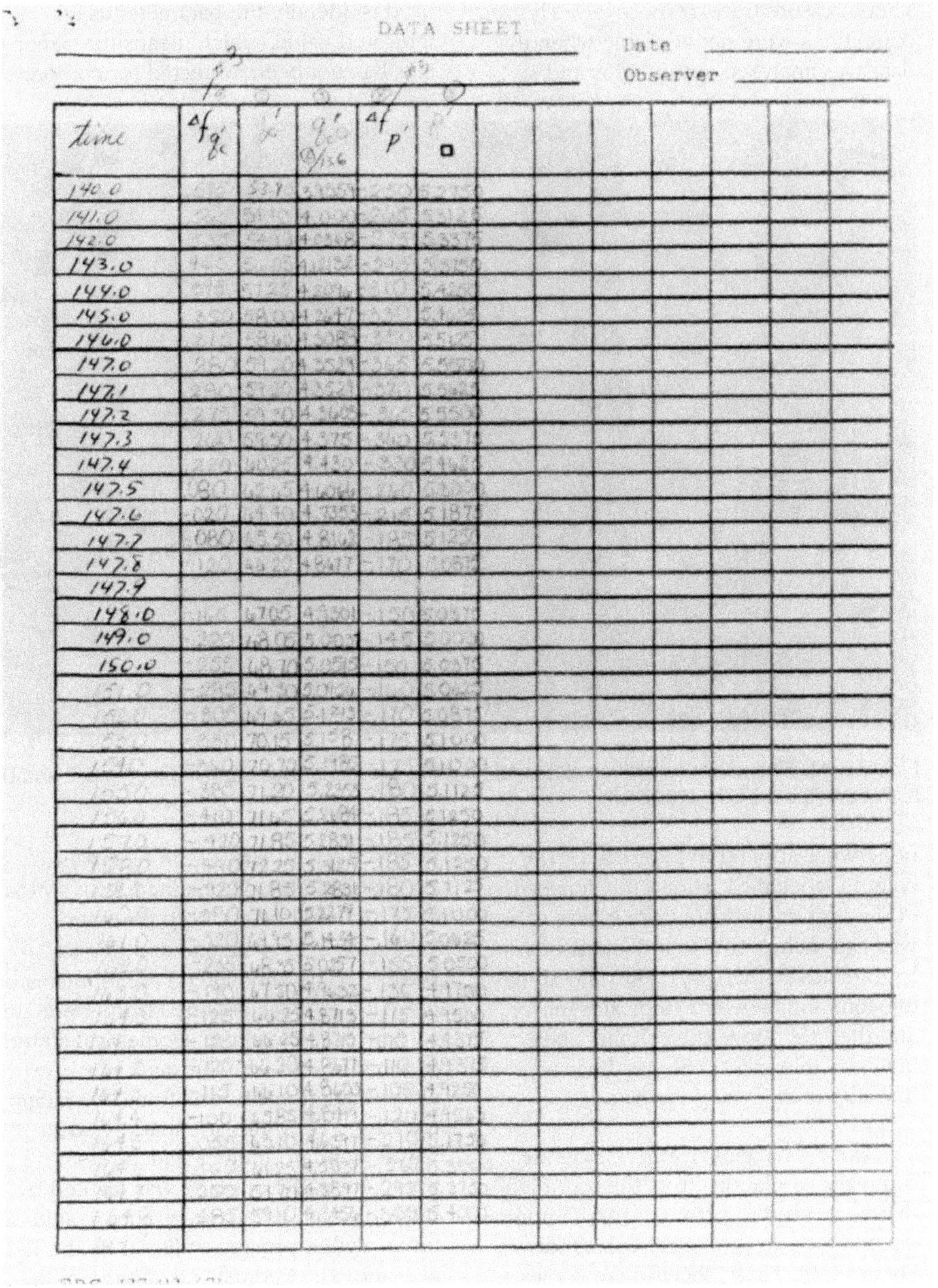

† The zero readings were obtained before and after the flight (as near as practically possible to the takeoff and landing) for a "known" value. If necessary, the "zero" deflection would then be adjusted so that the value read from the calibration curve was the same as the "known" value. The difference was always the average of the preflight and postflight values unless one of them was unavailable. This difference was then applied to the values read from the film.

†† Because an instrument was calibrated several times during a flight program, each calibration plot was only used for designated flights. This plot for film deflection versus absolute pressure was dated 31 December 1947. The plot area measured 13 by 30 inches and film deflection in inches ranged, bottom to top, from -0.8 to 1.8 and absolute pressure in inches of mercury, left to right, from 31 to 1 (also see note p. 61). This calibration was run for temperatures of 0° and 80° Fahrenheit. Increasing and decreasing pressure values were taken at approximately the same deflections. Thus values for a given deflection were near the same point on the paper. Rather than overlap, the symbols were offset from the curve and lines drawn to the actual value. The non-sensitive trace curve, seen crossing the mirror curves, aided in mirror identification as a mirror went off-scale, or out of its calibrated pressure range, and the next mirror trace appeared on the film. [The non-sensitive trace was also referred to as coarse or follow-on trace; discussions with Lannie (Dean) Webb, Edwin Saltzman and Roy G. Bryant on 21 January 1997.]

Figure B-10. Example data sheet showing hand recorded film deflections. (NASA Photo EC93 42307-37)

As the film was read (at least before the computer age), the deflections at the desired times were written on a sheet. Figure B-10 shows a representative sheet. The mirror number for those traces with more than one mirror was also recorded. After the film was read, the film readings were adjusted for preflight and postflight zero readings.† Then the zero-corrected readings were used with a calibration plot to obtain the pressure. Figure B-11 shows a five mirror calibration plot. Mirror 1 is on the left, and mirror 5 is on the right. This plot is the calibration curve†† that would be used for the static pressure trace shown in Figure B-8 [$\Delta f_p'$ on the sheet shown in Figures. B-9 (a) and B-10]. The data sheets shown in Figure B-9 (a) were compiled from the film shown in Figures B-2 and B-8. The $\Delta f_{qc}'$ (column labeled "1") and the $\Delta f_p'$ (column labeled "4") headings refer to the impact pressure trace and the

51

static pressure trace, respectively. The zero corrections were not available when this data was analyzed in the 1970s and so

used to identify the parameter as an indicated value, which means the parameter has not been corrected for compress-

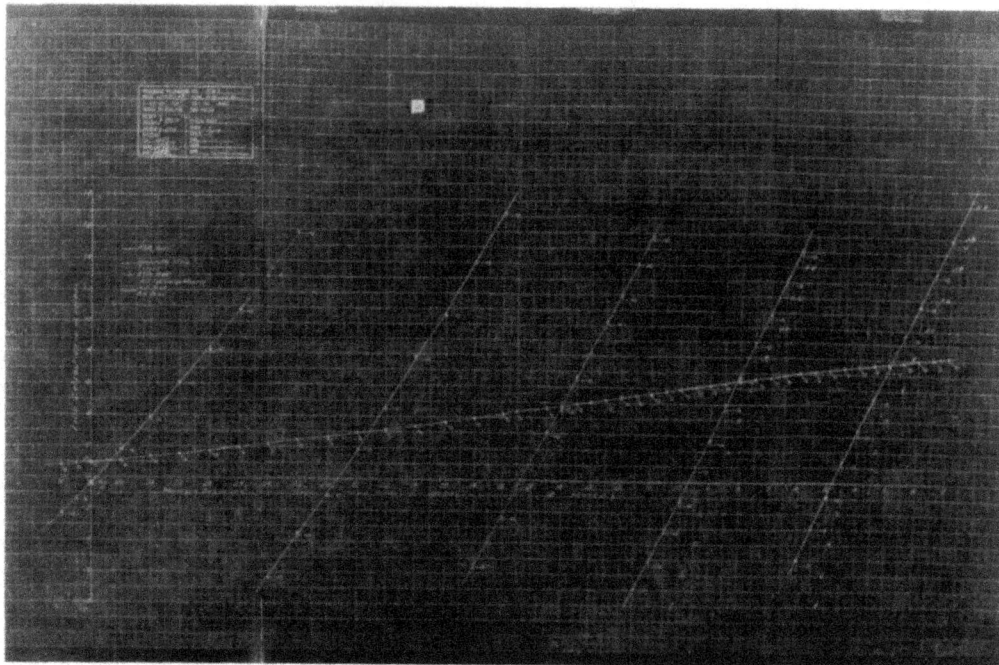

Figure B-11. Five mirror calibration plot used for static pressure trace seen in Figures B-7 and B-8. (NASA Photo EC93 42307-28)

none were applied to these data.[†] The column labeled "3" shows the conversion of the impact pressure from inches of water to inches of mercury (static pressure is in inches of mercury). The "#3" above the column labeled "1" indicates mirror 3 and the "#5" above the column labeled "4" indicates mirror 5. These readings were a first step in analyzing the data.

The data sheets in Figure B-12 are summary tabulations from the four flights that were used to obtain the Mach number error curve (position error curve) shown in Figure B-13. These sheets were copies made by Roxanah Yancey from the original sheets. As can be seen, a number of calculations were needed before the final answers were obtained. The sheets all have the data in the same order, but only the sheets for flight 5 [figs. B-12 (a) and (b)] have numbers above the columns. Because these were summary sheets, the film deflections and zero corrections were not included. The columns labeled "3" and "5" in Figures B-12 (a) and (b) correspond to the columns labeled "5" and "3," respectively, for the data sheet in Figure B-10.[††] The "prime" (for example, P'_H) was

ibility effects.[†††] H_{Radar}, in feet, was a geometrical altitude obtained from a radar track of the airplane. Both the static pressures (P parameters) and impact pressures (q_c parameters) are in inches of mercury. P_H was obtained from a pressure survey that related the geometrical altitude to a static pressure. The static pressure and altitude relationship was found by radar-tracking a B-29 airplane that towed a NACA standard trailing static-pressure bomb.[‡] The X-1 airplane was tracked by radar through the same geometric-altitude range as that previously flown by the B-29 airplane. The geometrical altitude of the X-1 airplane was then used to determine P_H. M' (column 7) was obtained from tables[#] using the values in column 6, and M (column 10) was obtained from a table using the values in column 9. Figure B-12 (b) shows the equations for the parameters in columns 4, 8, and 11. The P' in the denominator of column 6 is the P'_H value in column 3 and the P in the denominator of column 9 is the P_H value in column 2.

The data sheets (figs. B-10 and B-12) indicate the effort required to obtain the data plot shown in Figure B-13. The values

[†] These data were used to identify the film, and although desirable, the zeros were not necessary to identify the film.

[††] These values from figure B-10 are from flight 9 and correspond to the values for flight 9 in Figures B-12 (e) and (f). The values in the two figures are different (for example, the values for time 147.4) because zero corrections were not applied to the film deflections in figure B-10.

[†††] Compressibility is the property of air by virtue of which the density increases with increase in pressure. This property is manifested at speeds approaching that of sound and higher. In practical terms, compressibility means that the density changes in the air can no longer be neglected and that corrections must be applied to these pressures.

[‡] Harold R. Goodman and Roxanah B. Yancey, *The Static-Pressure Error of Wing and Fuselage Airspeed Installations of the X-1 Airplanes in Transonic Flight* (Washington, D.C.: NACA RM L9G22, 1949).

[#] One such table is found in: Ames Research Staff, *Equations, Tables, and Charts for Compressibility Flow* (Washington, D.C.: NACA TR-1135, 1953). This replaced NACA TN-1428 from 1947.

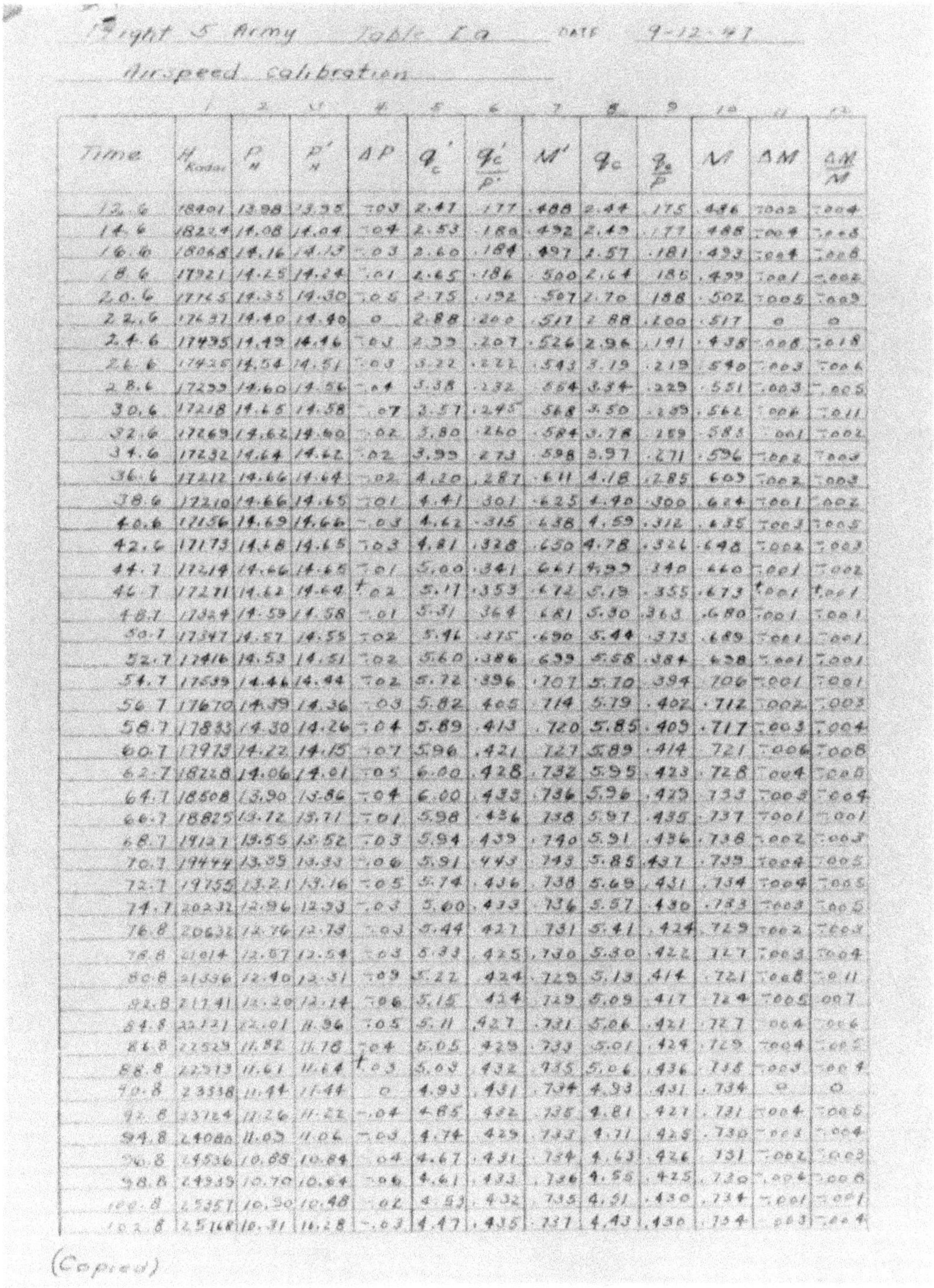

Flight 5 Army   Table I.a   DATE 9-12-47

Airspeed calibration

	1	2	3	4	5	6	7	8	9	10	11	12
Time	H_{Radar}	P_M	P'_M	ΔP	q_c'	$\dfrac{q_c'}{P'}$	M'	q_c	$\dfrac{q_c}{P}$	M	ΔM	$\dfrac{\Delta M}{M}$
12.6	18401	13.98	13.95	-.03	2.47	.177	.488	2.44	.175	.486	-.002	-.004
14.6	18224	14.08	14.04	-.04	2.53	.180	.492	2.49	.177	.488	-.004	-.008
16.6	18068	14.16	14.13	-.03	2.60	.184	.497	2.57	.181	.493	-.004	-.008
18.6	17921	14.25	14.24	-.01	2.65	.186	.500	2.64	.185	.499	-.001	-.002
20.6	17745	14.35	14.30	-.05	2.75	.192	.507	2.70	.188	.502	-.005	-.009
22.6	17637	14.40	14.40	0	2.88	.200	.517	2.88	.200	.517	0	0
24.6	17435	14.17	14.16	-.01	3.33	.207	.526	2.96	.191	.538	-.008	-.018
26.6	17425	14.54	14.51	-.03	3.22	.221	.543	3.19	.219	.540	-.003	-.006
28.6	17253	14.60	14.56	-.04	3.38	.232	.554	3.34	.229	.551	-.003	-.005
30.6	17218	14.65	14.58	-.07	3.57	.245	.568	3.50	.239	.562	-.006	-.011
32.6	17263	14.62	14.60	-.02	3.80	.260	.584	3.78	.259	.583	-.001	-.002
34.6	17232	14.64	14.62	-.02	3.99	.273	.598	3.97	.271	.596	-.002	-.003
36.6	17212	14.66	14.64	-.02	4.20	.287	.611	4.18	.285	.609	-.002	-.003
38.6	17210	14.66	14.65	-.01	4.41	.301	.625	4.40	.300	.624	-.001	-.002
40.6	17156	14.69	14.66	-.03	4.62	.315	.638	4.59	.312	.635	-.003	-.005
42.6	17173	14.68	14.65	-.03	4.81	.328	.650	4.78	.326	.648	-.002	-.003
44.7	17219	14.66	14.65	-.01	5.00	.341	.661	4.99	.340	.660	-.001	-.002
46.7	17271	14.62	14.64	+.02	5.17	.353	.672	5.19	.355	.673	+.001	+.001
48.7	17324	14.59	14.58	-.01	5.31	.364	.681	5.30	.363	.680	-.001	-.001
50.7	17347	14.57	14.55	-.02	5.46	.375	.690	5.44	.373	.689	-.001	-.001
52.7	17416	14.53	14.51	-.02	5.60	.386	.699	5.58	.384	.698	-.001	-.001
54.7	17559	14.46	14.44	-.02	5.72	.396	.707	5.70	.394	.706	-.001	-.001
56.7	17670	14.39	14.36	-.03	5.82	.405	.714	5.79	.402	.712	-.002	-.003
58.7	17833	14.30	14.26	-.04	5.89	.413	.720	5.85	.409	.717	-.003	-.004
60.7	17973	14.22	14.15	-.07	5.96	.421	.727	5.89	.414	.721	-.006	-.008
62.7	18228	14.06	14.01	-.05	6.00	.428	.732	5.95	.423	.728	-.004	-.008
64.7	18508	13.90	13.86	-.04	6.00	.432	.736	5.96	.429	.733	-.003	-.004
66.7	18825	13.72	13.71	-.01	5.98	.436	.738	5.97	.435	.737	-.001	-.001
68.7	19127	13.55	13.52	-.03	5.94	.439	.740	5.91	.436	.738	-.002	-.003
70.7	19474	13.35	13.33	-.02	5.91	.443	.743	5.85	.437	.739	-.004	-.005
72.7	19755	13.21	13.16	-.05	5.74	.436	.738	5.69	.431	.734	-.004	-.005
74.7	20232	12.96	12.93	-.03	5.60	.433	.736	5.57	.430	.733	-.003	-.005
76.8	20632	12.76	12.73	-.03	5.44	.427	.731	5.41	.424	.729	-.002	-.003
78.8	21014	12.57	12.54	-.03	5.33	.425	.730	5.30	.422	.727	-.003	-.004
80.8	21336	12.40	12.31	-.09	5.22	.424	.729	5.13	.414	.721	-.008	-.011
82.8	21741	12.20	12.14	-.06	5.15	.424	.729	5.09	.417	.724	-.005	-.007
84.8	22121	12.01	11.96	-.05	5.11	.427	.731	5.06	.421	.727	-.004	-.006
86.8	22529	11.82	11.78	-.04	5.05	.429	.733	5.01	.424	.729	-.004	-.005
88.8	22913	11.61	11.64	+.03	5.03	.432	.735	5.06	.436	.738	-.003	-.004
90.8	23338	11.44	11.44	0	4.93	.431	.734	4.93	.431	.734	0	0
92.8	23724	11.26	11.22	-.04	4.85	.432	.735	4.81	.427	.731	-.004	-.005
94.8	24080	11.09	11.06	-.03	4.74	.429	.733	4.71	.425	.730	-.003	-.004
96.8	24536	10.88	10.84	-.04	4.67	.431	.734	4.63	.426	.731	-.002	-.003
98.8	24915	10.70	10.64	-.06	4.61	.433	.736	4.55	.425	.730	-.004	-.006
100.8	25351	10.50	10.48	-.02	4.53	.432	.735	4.51	.430	.734	-.001	-.001
102.8	25768	10.31	10.28	-.03	4.47	.435	.737	4.43	.430	.734	-.003	-.004

(Copied)

Figure B-12 (a) Flight 5, 12 September 1947. (NASA Photo EC93 42307-29)

Figure B-12. Data sheets used to obtain Mach number error curve from flights leading to and including first piloted aircraft, XS-1 #1, to exceed the speed of sound.

plotted from the data sheets of Figure B-12 are the Mach number, M, from column 10 and the Mach number error, ΔM/M, from column 12. The plotted data show the variation of the error in Mach number as a function of the corrected Mach number (often referred to as the true Mach number). The abrupt change in the data values at a Mach number of 1 is called the Mach jump. A positive ΔM/M means the corrected (or true) Mach number is larger than indicated Mach number and a negative ΔM/M means indicated Mach number is larger than the corrected Mach number. The data show that for Mach numbers from 0.88 to approximately 1.02,

53

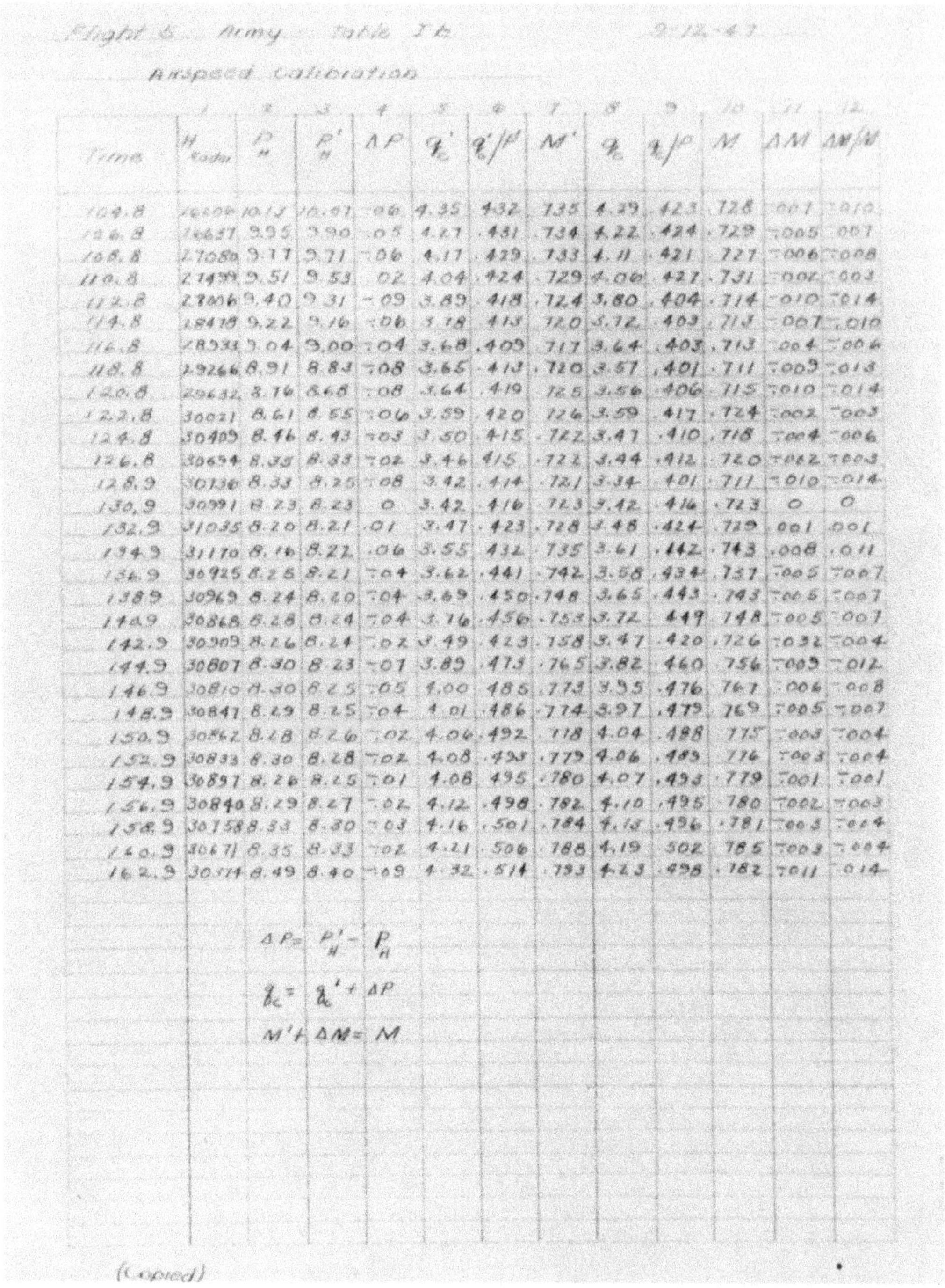

Flight 5 Army Table I b 9-12-47

Airspeed calibration

	1	2	3	4	5	6	7	8	9	10	11	12
Time	H_{Radar}	P_H	P'_H	ΔP	q'_c	q'_c/P	M'	q_c	q_c/P	M	ΔM	$\Delta M/M$
104.8	26606	10.13	10.07	-.06	4.35	.432	.735	4.29	.423	.728	-.007	-.010
106.8	26637	9.95	9.90	-.05	4.27	.431	.734	4.22	.424	.729	-.005	-.007
108.8	27080	9.77	9.71	-.06	4.17	.429	.733	4.11	.421	.727	-.006	-.008
110.8	27499	9.51	9.53	.02	4.04	.424	.729	4.06	.427	.731	-.002	-.003
112.8	28006	9.40	9.31	-.09	3.89	.418	.724	3.80	.404	.714	-.010	-.014
114.8	28478	9.22	9.16	-.06	3.78	.413	.720	3.72	.403	.713	-.007	-.010
116.8	28933	9.04	9.00	-.04	3.68	.409	.717	3.64	.403	.713	-.004	-.006
118.8	29266	8.91	8.83	-.08	3.65	.413	.720	3.57	.401	.711	-.009	-.013
120.8	29632	8.76	8.68	-.08	3.64	.419	.725	3.56	.406	.715	-.010	-.014
122.8	30021	8.61	8.55	-.06	3.59	.420	.726	3.59	.417	.724	-.002	-.003
124.8	30409	8.46	8.43	-.03	3.50	.415	.722	3.47	.410	.718	-.004	-.006
126.8	30634	8.35	8.33	-.02	3.46	.415	.722	3.44	.412	.720	-.002	-.003
128.9	30736	8.33	8.25	-.08	3.42	.414	.721	3.34	.401	.711	-.010	-.014
130.9	30991	8.23	8.23	0	3.42	.416	.723	3.42	.416	.723	0	0
132.9	31035	8.20	8.21	.01	3.47	.423	.728	3.48	.424	.729	.001	.001
134.9	31170	8.16	8.22	.06	3.55	.432	.735	3.61	.442	.743	.008	.011
136.9	30925	8.25	8.21	-.04	3.62	.441	.742	3.58	.434	.737	-.005	-.007
138.9	30969	8.24	8.20	-.04	3.69	.450	.748	3.65	.443	.743	-.005	-.007
140.9	30868	8.28	8.24	-.04	3.76	.456	.753	3.72	.449	.748	-.005	-.007
142.9	30909	8.26	8.24	-.02	3.49	.423	.758	3.47	.420	.726	-.032	-.004
144.9	30807	8.30	8.23	-.07	3.89	.473	.765	3.82	.460	.756	-.009	-.012
146.9	30810	8.30	8.25	-.05	4.00	.485	.773	3.95	.476	.767	-.006	-.008
148.9	30847	8.29	8.25	-.04	4.01	.486	.774	3.97	.479	.769	-.005	-.007
150.9	30862	8.28	8.26	-.02	4.06	.492	.778	4.04	.488	.775	-.003	-.004
152.9	30833	8.30	8.28	-.02	4.08	.493	.779	4.06	.489	.776	-.003	-.004
154.9	30897	8.26	8.25	-.01	4.08	.495	.780	4.07	.493	.779	-.001	-.001
156.9	30840	8.29	8.27	-.02	4.12	.498	.782	4.10	.495	.780	-.002	-.003
158.9	30758	8.33	8.30	-.03	4.16	.501	.784	4.13	.496	.781	-.003	-.004
160.9	30671	8.35	8.33	-.02	4.21	.506	.788	4.19	.502	.785	-.003	-.004
162.9	30574	8.49	8.40	-.09	4.32	.514	.793	4.23	.498	.782	-.011	-.014

$\Delta P = P'_H - P_H$

$q_c = q'_c + \Delta P$

$M' + \Delta M = M$

(Copied)

Figure B-12 (b) Flight 5, 12 September 1947, concluded. (NASA Photo EC93 42307-32)

the indicated Mach number (the Mach number seen during the flight) was indicating the aircraft speed was slower than it actually was. For Mach numbers greater than approximately 1.02, the indicated Mach number was indicating the aircraft speed was faster then it actually was.

The Mach number error curve (position error curve) in Figure B-13† was used in calibrating the nose boom of the X-1. The curve obtained from the data of X-1 flights 5, 7, and 8 [figs. B-12 (a) through (d)] was used to determine what the indicated Mach number had to be in order for the airplane to be flown at a Mach number greater than 1. Flight 9 extended the calibration to Mach numbers greater than 1. Thus, Figure B-13 represents the position error curve for the "buildup" flights and the first flight to exceed the sound barrier.

† The fold line in this plot exists because the plotting paper was 11 by 17 inches (the "lined" part being 10 by 15 inches). Any plot page that was larger than 8 1/2 by 11 inches would eventually be folded to fit in an 8 1/2 by 11 inch storage area such as a notebook or manilla folder

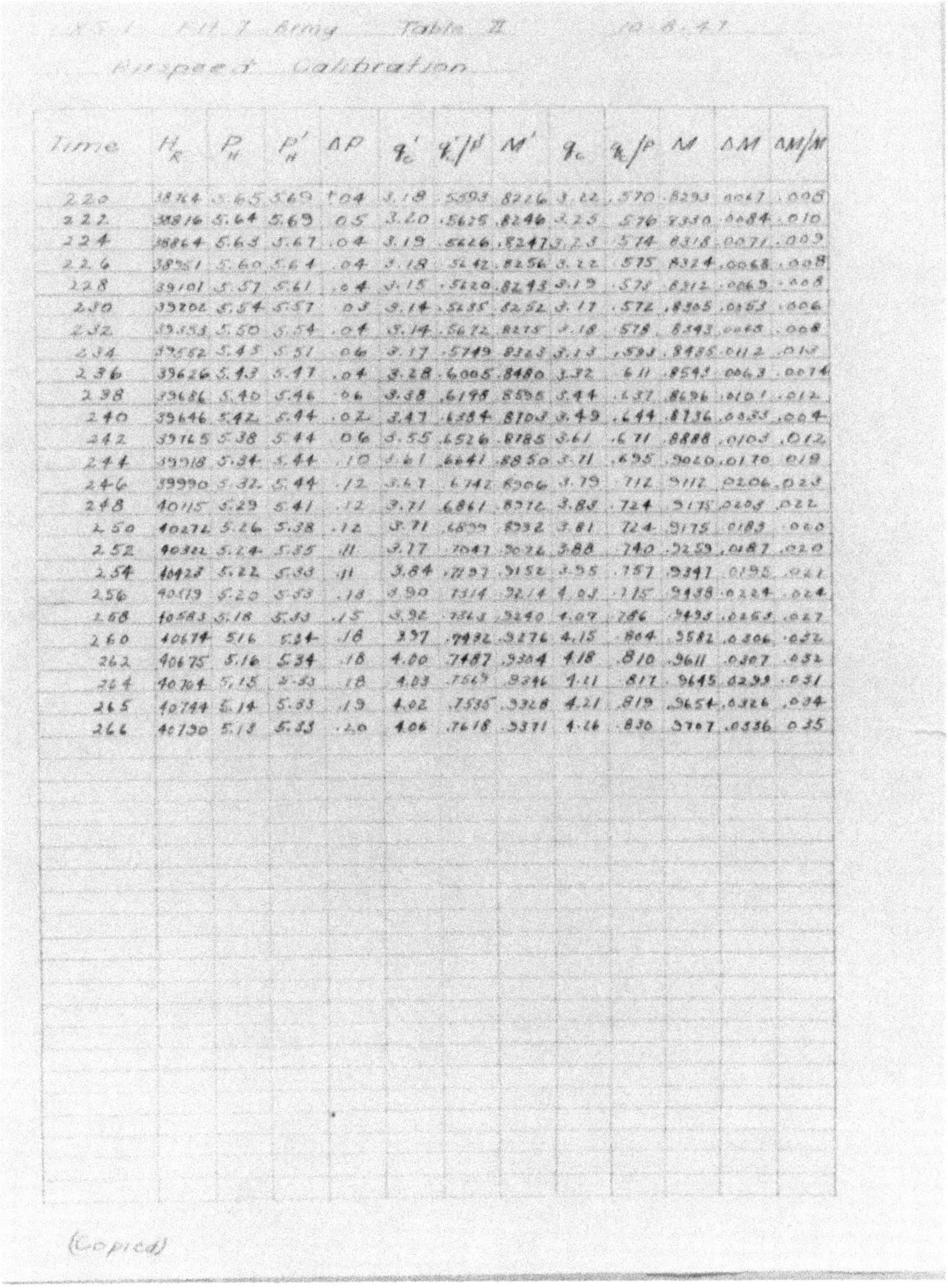

Airspeed Calibration

Time	H_R	P_H	P_H'	ΔP	q_c'	q_c'/p	M'	q_c	q_c/p	M	ΔM	$\Delta M/M$
2.20	38764	5.65	5.69	+.04	3.18	.5593	.8226	3.22	.570	.8293	.0067	.008
2.22	38816	5.64	5.69	.05	3.20	.5635	.8246	3.25	.576	.8330	.0084	.010
2.24	38864	5.63	5.67	.04	3.19	.5626	.8247	3.23	.574	.8318	.0071	.009
2.26	38951	5.60	5.64	.04	3.18	.5642	.8256	3.22	.575	.8324	.0068	.008
2.28	39101	5.57	5.61	.04	3.15	.5620	.8243	3.19	.578	.8312	.0069	.008
2.30	39202	5.54	5.57	.03	3.14	.5685	.8252	3.17	.572	.8305	.0053	.006
2.32	39353	5.50	5.54	.04	3.14	.5672	.8275	3.18	.578	.8343	.0068	.008
2.34	39552	5.45	5.51	.06	3.17	.5749	.8365	3.23	.593	.8485	.0112	.013
2.36	39626	5.43	5.47	.04	3.28	.6005	.8480	3.32	.611	.8543	.0063	.0074
2.38	39686	5.40	5.46	.06	3.38	.6195	.8585	3.44	.637	.8696	.0101	.012
2.40	39646	5.42	5.44	.02	3.47	.6384	.8703	3.49	.644	.8736	.0033	.004
2.42	39765	5.38	5.44	.06	3.55	.6526	.8785	3.61	.671	.8888	.0103	.012
2.44	39918	5.34	5.44	.10	3.61	.6641	.8850	3.71	.695	.9020	.0170	.019
2.46	39990	5.32	5.44	.12	3.67	.6742	.8906	3.79	.712	.9112	.0206	.023
2.48	40115	5.29	5.41	.12	3.71	.6861	.8972	3.83	.724	.9175	.0208	.022
2.50	40272	5.26	5.38	.12	3.71	.6899	.8992	3.81	.724	.9175	.0183	.060
2.52	40302	5.24	5.35	.11	3.77	.7047	.9072	3.88	.740	.9259	.0187	.020
2.54	40423	5.22	5.33	.11	3.84	.7197	.9152	3.95	.757	.9347	.0195	.021
2.56	40419	5.20	5.33	.14	3.90	.7314	.9214	4.03	.775	.9438	.0224	.024
2.58	40543	5.18	5.33	.15	3.96	.7463	.9290	4.07	.786	.9493	.0263	.027
2.60	40674	5.16	5.34	.18	3.97	.7492	.9276	4.15	.804	.9582	.0306	.032
2.62	40675	5.16	5.34	.18	4.00	.7487	.9304	4.18	.810	.9611	.0307	.032
2.64	40704	5.15	5.33	.18	4.03	.7569	.9346	4.11	.817	.9645	.0299	.031
2.65	40744	5.14	5.33	.19	4.02	.7535	.9328	4.21	.819	.9654	.0326	.034
2.66	40730	5.13	5.33	.20	4.06	.7618	.9371	4.24	.830	.9707	.0336	.035

(Copied)

Figure B-12 (c) Flight 7, 8 October 1947. (NASA Photo EC93 42307-30)

Figure B-14 is a composite showing the data sheets, calibration curve, final curve, and some of the tools used in plotting. The 8 1/2-inch wide by 11-inch long data sheets give an idea of the size of the calibration curve plot. By the time the final plots were obtained, the person working with the data was very familiar with and knowledgeable about every data point. The digital computers of today have certainly eliminated the time-consuming and tedious workup of the data, but they have also eliminated the extremely close familiarity that the engineer used to have with the data.

Film Reading and Plotting Tools

Figure B-15 shows a sample of the tools used by the women computers and the engineers. Standard issue equipment for the women computers was a lightbox,

55

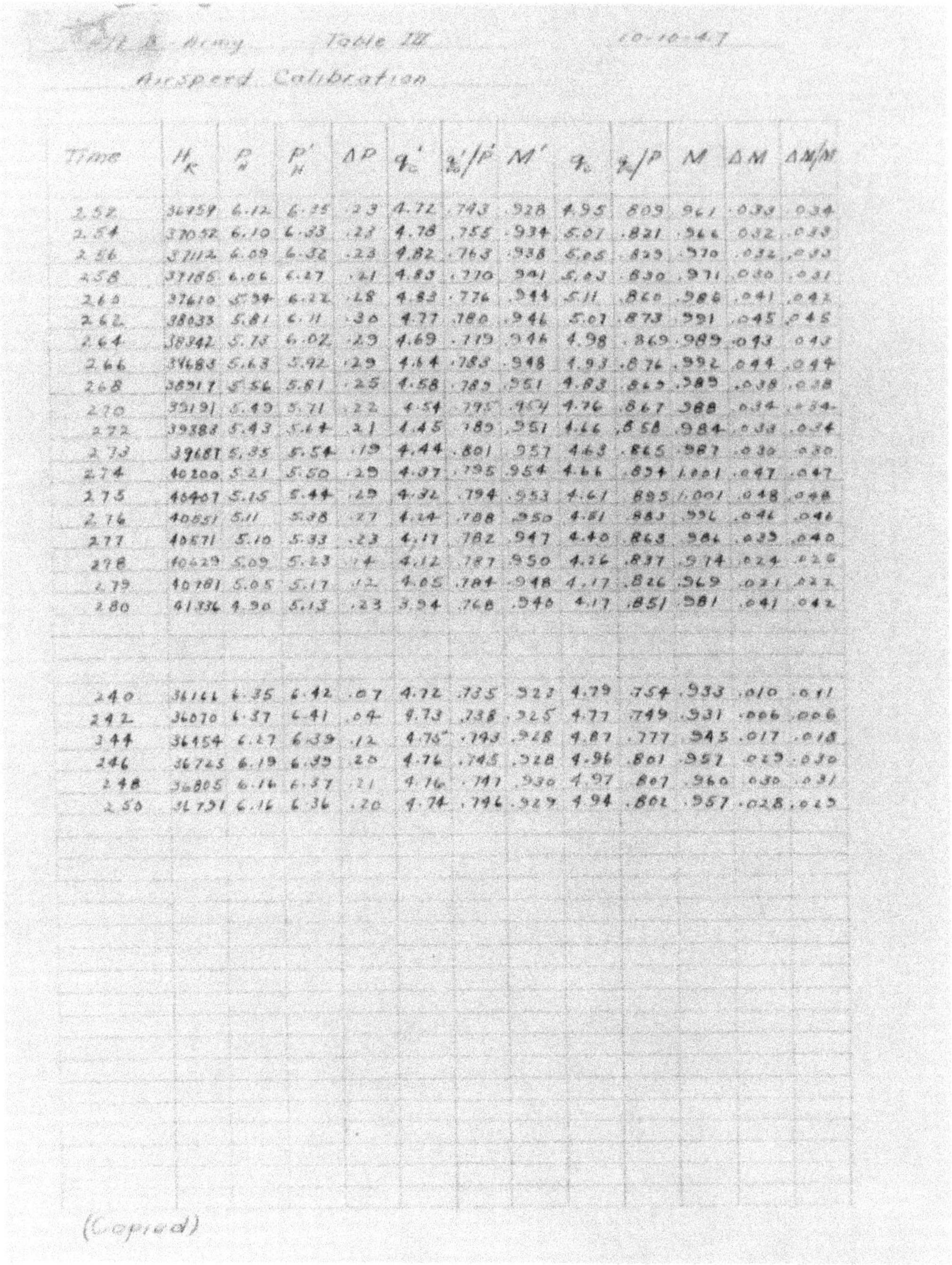

XLR Army Table IX 10-10-47

Airspeed Calibration

Time	H_K	P_H	P'_H	ΔP	q'_c	q'_c/P'	M'	q_c	q_c/P	M	ΔM	$\Delta M/M$
252	36959	6.12	6.35	.23	4.72	.743	.928	4.95	.809	.961	.033	.034
254	37052	6.10	6.33	.23	4.78	.755	.934	5.01	.821	.966	.032	.033
256	37112	6.09	6.32	.23	4.82	.763	.938	5.05	.829	.970	.032	.033
258	37185	6.06	6.27	.21	4.83	.770	.941	5.03	.830	.971	.030	.031
260	37610	5.94	6.22	.28	4.83	.776	.944	5.11	.860	.986	.041	.042
262	38033	5.81	6.11	.30	4.77	.780	.946	5.07	.873	.991	.045	.045
264	38342	5.73	6.02	.29	4.69	.779	.946	4.98	.869	.989	.043	.043
266	38683	5.63	5.92	.29	4.64	.783	.948	4.93	.876	.992	.044	.044
268	38917	5.56	5.81	.25	4.58	.789	.951	4.83	.869	.989	.038	.038
270	39191	5.49	5.71	.22	4.54	.795	.954	4.76	.867	.988	.034	.034
272	39388	5.43	5.64	.21	4.45	.789	.951	4.66	.858	.984	.033	.034
273	39681	5.35	5.54	.19	4.44	.801	.957	4.63	.865	.987	.030	.030
274	40200	5.21	5.50	.29	4.37	.795	.954	4.66	.894	1.001	.047	.047
275	40407	5.15	5.44	.29	4.32	.794	.953	4.61	.895	1.001	.048	.048
276	40551	5.11	5.38	.27	4.24	.788	.950	4.51	.883	.996	.046	.046
277	40571	5.10	5.33	.23	4.17	.782	.947	4.40	.863	.986	.039	.040
278	40629	5.09	5.23	.14	4.12	.787	.950	4.26	.837	.974	.024	.026
279	40781	5.05	5.17	.12	4.05	.784	.948	4.17	.826	.969	.021	.022
280	41336	4.90	5.13	.23	3.94	.768	.940	4.17	.851	.981	.041	.042
240	36166	6.35	6.42	.07	4.72	.735	.923	4.79	.754	.933	.010	.011
242	36070	6.37	6.41	.04	4.73	.738	.925	4.77	.749	.931	.006	.006
244	36154	6.27	6.39	.12	4.75	.743	.928	4.87	.777	.945	.017	.018
246	36725	6.19	6.39	.20	4.76	.745	.928	4.96	.801	.957	.029	.030
248	36805	6.16	6.37	.21	4.76	.747	.930	4.97	.807	.960	.030	.031
250	36731	6.16	6.36	.20	4.74	.746	.929	4.94	.802	.957	.028	.029

(Copied)

Figure B-12 (d) Flight 8, 10 October 1947. (NASA Photo EC93 42307-31)

Friden automatic calculator, eraser shield, magnifying glass, symbol maker, film scale, and triangles.† The magnifying glass [fig. B-15 (a)] and the film scale [fig. B-15 (b)] were used extensively in film reading. Some people even used makeshift stands to hold the magnifying glass at the right height above the film so their hands could be free to position the film scale and record the deflections.†† The magnifying glass was also useful in reading data points from calibration curves or other plots.

Because equipment, such as the magnifying glass and the film scale, was difficult to acquire, people would put their name or other identification on it. Some of the equipment, at least in the early days, even had to be checked out. The box for the magnifying glass has NACA Muroc Computer #3 written on it [fig. B-15 (a)]. The name on the handle of the magnifying glass, Roxanah Yancey, was added sometime later. The film scales were also tightly controlled. When I first started working, I

† Recollections of Betty Scott Love, 3 August 1994.

†† The film scales were purchased in lots from the Dietzgen Company. A serious attempt was made to have all film scales bought from the same lot in order to avoid uncertainty or arguments about "non-sanctioned" scales.

† I don't know what they cost, but I do know it was not easy to have a personal film scale.

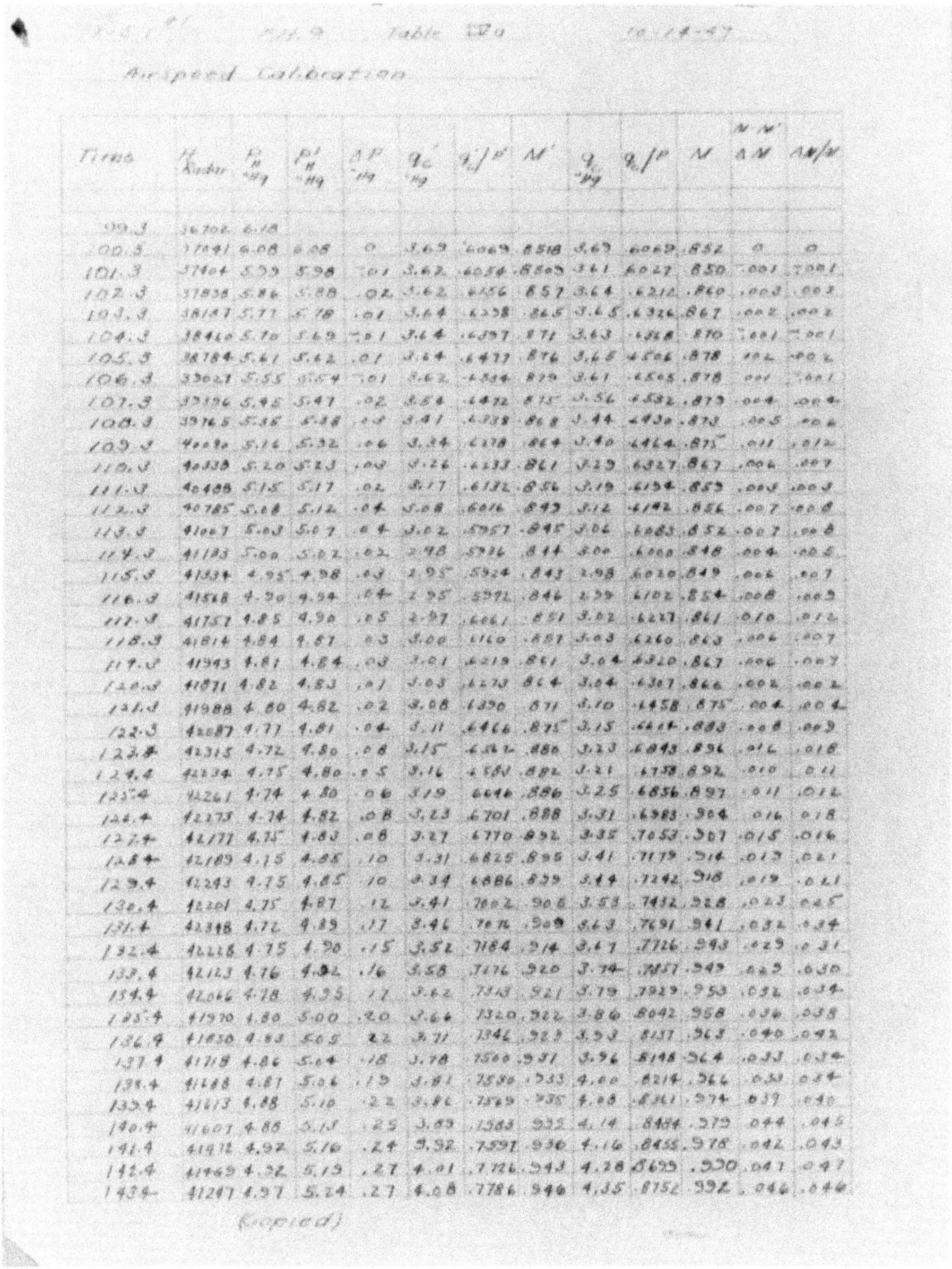

X-S-1 #1 Flt. 9 Table IVa 10-14-47

Airspeed Calibration

Time	H Radar	P_H "Hg	P'_H "Hg	ΔP "Hg	q'_c "Hg	q'_c/P	M'	q_c "Hg	q_c/P	M	M-M' ΔM	ΔM/M
99.3	36702	6.18										
100.3	37041	6.08	6.08	0	3.69	.6069	.8518	3.69	.6069	.852	0	0
101.3	37404	5.99	5.98	-.01	3.62	.6054	.8505	3.61	.6027	.850	-.001	-.001
102.3	37838	5.86	5.88	.02	3.62	.6156	.857	3.64	.6212	.860	.003	.003
103.3	38187	5.77	5.78	.01	3.64	.6298	.865	3.65	.6326	.867	.002	.002
104.3	38460	5.70	5.69	-.01	3.64	.6397	.871	3.63	.6368	.870	-.001	-.001
105.3	38784	5.61	5.62	.01	3.64	.6477	.876	3.65	.6506	.878	.002	.002
106.3	39021	5.55	5.54	-.01	3.62	.6534	.879	3.61	.6505	.878	.001	-.001
107.3	39396	5.45	5.47	.02	3.54	.6472	.875	3.56	.6532	.879	.004	.004
108.3	39765	5.38	5.34	.04	3.41	.6338	.868	3.44	.6430	.873	.005	.006
109.3	40090	5.16	5.32	.06	3.34	.6278	.864	3.40	.6464	.875	.011	.012
110.3	40339	5.20	5.23	.03	3.26	.6233	.861	3.29	.6327	.867	.006	.007
111.3	40488	5.15	5.17	.02	3.17	.6132	.856	3.19	.6194	.859	.003	.003
112.3	40785	5.08	5.12	.04	3.08	.6016	.849	3.12	.6142	.856	.007	.008
113.3	41007	5.03	5.07	.04	3.02	.5957	.845	3.06	.6083	.852	.007	.008
114.3	41183	5.00	5.02	.02	2.98	.5936	.844	3.00	.6000	.848	.004	.005
115.3	41334	4.95	4.98	.03	2.95	.5924	.843	2.98	.6020	.849	.006	.007
116.3	41568	4.90	4.94	.04	2.95	.5972	.846	2.99	.6102	.854	.008	.009
117.3	41757	4.85	4.90	.05	2.97	.6061	.851	3.02	.6227	.861	.010	.012
118.3	41814	4.84	4.87	.03	3.00	.6160	.857	3.03	.6260	.863	.006	.007
119.3	41943	4.81	4.84	.03	3.01	.6219	.861	3.04	.6320	.867	.006	.007
120.3	41871	4.82	4.83	.01	3.03	.6273	.864	3.04	.6307	.866	.002	.002
121.3	41988	4.80	4.82	.02	3.08	.6390	.871	3.10	.6458	.875	.004	.004
122.3	42087	4.77	4.81	.04	3.11	.6466	.875	3.15	.6614	.883	.008	.009
123.4	42315	4.72	4.80	.08	3.15	.6562	.880	3.23	.6843	.896	.016	.018
124.4	42234	4.75	4.80	.05	3.16	.6583	.882	3.21	.6738	.892	.010	.011
125.4	42261	4.74	4.80	.06	3.19	.6646	.886	3.25	.6856	.897	.011	.012
126.4	42273	4.74	4.82	.08	3.23	.6701	.888	3.31	.6983	.904	.016	.018
127.4	42177	4.75	4.83	.08	3.27	.6770	.892	3.35	.7053	.907	.015	.016
128.4	42189	4.75	4.85	.10	3.31	.6825	.895	3.41	.7179	.914	.019	.021
129.4	42243	4.75	4.85	.10	3.34	.6886	.899	3.44	.7242	.918	.019	.021
130.4	42201	4.75	4.87	.12	3.41	.7002	.906	3.53	.7432	.928	.023	.025
131.4	42348	4.72	4.89	.17	3.46	.7076	.909	3.63	.7691	.941	.032	.034
132.4	42228	4.75	4.90	.15	3.52	.7184	.914	3.67	.7726	.943	.029	.031
133.4	42123	4.76	4.92	.16	3.58	.7276	.920	3.74	.7857	.949	.029	.030
134.4	42066	4.78	4.95	.17	3.62	.7313	.921	3.79	.7929	.953	.032	.034
135.4	41970	4.80	5.00	.20	3.66	.7320	.922	3.86	.8042	.958	.036	.038
136.4	41830	4.83	5.05	.22	3.71	.7346	.923	3.93	.8137	.963	.040	.042
137.4	41718	4.86	5.04	.18	3.78	.7500	.931	3.96	.8148	.964	.033	.034
138.4	41688	4.87	5.06	.19	3.81	.7530	.933	4.00	.8214	.966	.033	.034
139.4	41613	4.88	5.10	.22	3.86	.7569	.935	4.08	.8361	.974	.039	.040
140.4	41601	4.88	5.13	.25	3.89	.7565	.935	4.14	.8484	.979	.044	.045
141.4	41412	4.92	5.16	.24	3.92	.7591	.936	4.16	.8455	.978	.042	.043
142.4	41469	4.92	5.19	.27	4.01	.7726	.943	4.28	.8699	.990	.047	.047
143.4	41247	4.97	5.24	.27	4.08	.7786	.946	4.35	.8752	.992	.046	.046

(copied)

Figure B-12 (e) Flight 9, 14 October 1947. (NASA Photo EC93 42307-34)

had to borrow a film scale because they were too expensive for everyone to have one.† Most of the film could easily be read with a 6-inch scale, so that was the common size. Some of the film was wide enough to require a 12-inch scale. In order to save money, 12-inch scales were sometimes bought and cut in half to make two 6-inch scales because a 12-inch scale was cheaper than buying two 6-inch scales. The film scale shown in Figure B-15 (b) is half of a 12-inch scale.

Other equipment, such as the templates used to make symbols around data points (symbol makers) were also tightly controlled. Figure B-15 (b) shows the two sizes of symbol makers used most often. The light one shown in the figure was a clear, or transparent, plastic. The dark ones in the figure were also a transparent plastic but were an orange color. Sometimes a plot would be inked, and the tape on the symbol maker with the larger holes was to help keep the ink from smearing (at least

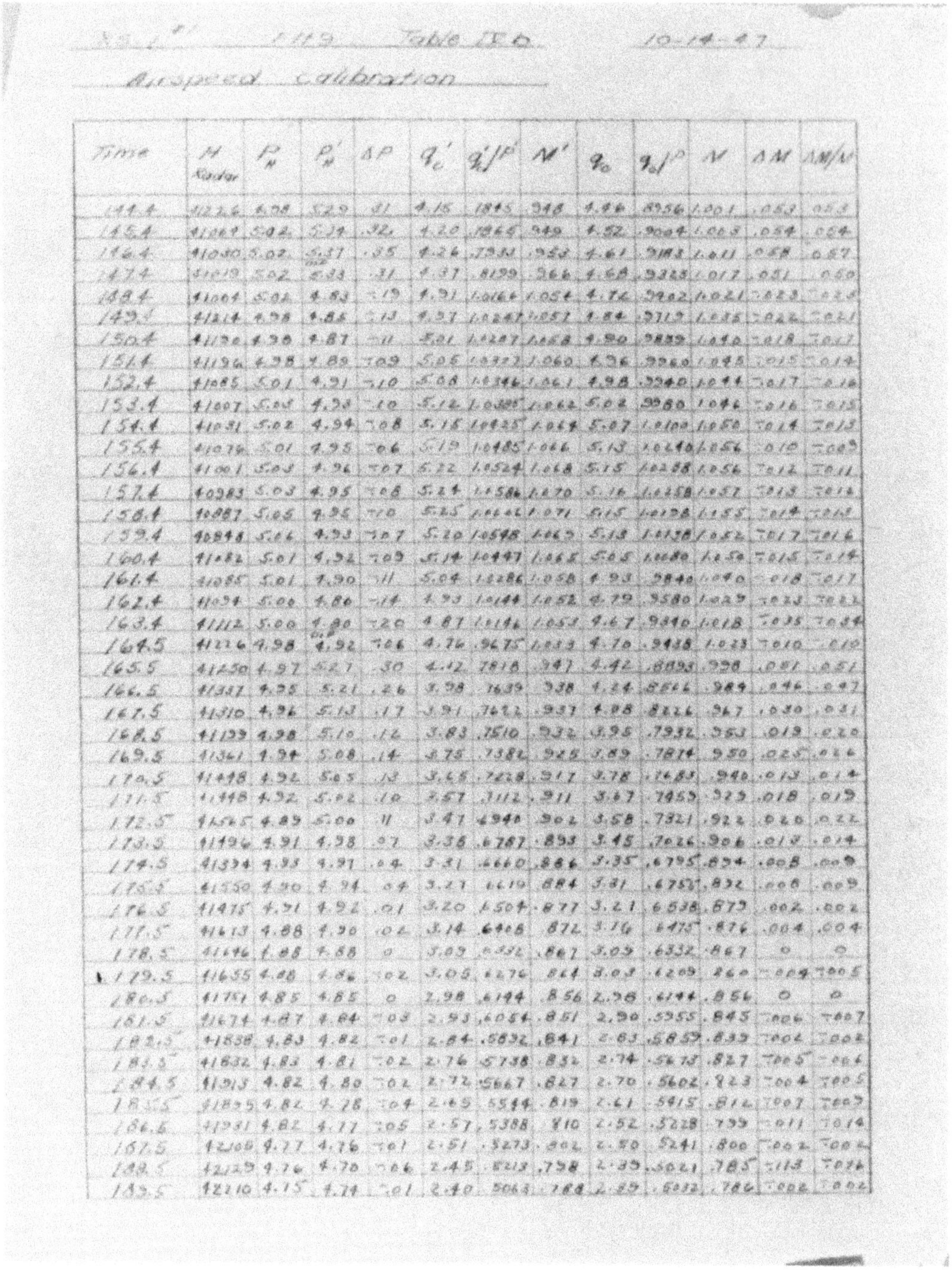

XS-1 #1 FL 9 Table IX a 10-14-47

Airspeed calibration

Time	M Radar	P_H	P'_H	ΔP	q'_c	q'_c/p	M'	q_c	q_c/p	M	ΔM	$\Delta M/M$
144.4	41226	5.08	5.29	.31	4.15	.8845	.948	4.46	.8956	1.001	.053	.053
145.4	41069	5.02	5.34	.32	4.20	.8865	.949	4.52	.9004	1.003	.054	.054
146.4	41030	5.02	5.37	.35	4.26	.7931	.953	4.61	.9183	1.011	.058	.057
147.4	41019	5.02	5.33	.31	4.37	.8199	.966	4.68	.9323	1.017	.051	.050
148.4	41004	5.02	4.83	-.19	4.91	1.0164	1.054	4.72	.9402	1.021	-.023	-.023
149.4	41214	4.98	4.86	-.13	4.97	1.0247	1.057	4.84	.9719	1.035	-.022	-.021
150.4	41170	4.98	4.87	-.11	5.01	1.0287	1.058	4.90	.9839	1.040	-.018	-.017
151.4	41196	4.98	4.89	-.09	5.05	1.0372	1.060	4.96	.9960	1.045	-.015	-.014
152.4	41085	5.01	4.91	-.10	5.08	1.0346	1.061	4.98	.9940	1.044	-.017	-.016
153.4	41007	5.04	4.94	-.10	5.14	1.0385	1.062	5.02	.9980	1.046	-.016	-.015
154.4	41031	5.02	4.94	-.08	5.15	1.0425	1.064	5.07	1.0100	1.050	-.014	-.013
155.4	41076	5.01	4.95	-.06	5.19	1.0485	1.066	5.13	1.0240	1.056	-.010	-.009
156.4	41001	5.03	4.96	-.07	5.22	1.0524	1.068	5.15	1.0288	1.056	-.012	-.011
157.4	40983	5.03	4.95	-.08	5.24	1.0586	1.070	5.16	1.0258	1.057	-.013	-.012
158.4	40887	5.05	4.95	-.10	5.25	1.0646	1.071	5.15	1.0198	1.055	-.014	-.013
159.4	40848	5.06	4.93	-.07	5.20	1.0548	1.065	5.13	1.0138	1.052	-.017	-.016
160.4	41082	5.01	4.92	-.09	5.14	1.0447	1.065	5.05	1.0080	1.050	-.015	-.014
161.4	41085	5.01	4.90	-.11	5.04	1.0286	1.058	4.93	.9840	1.040	-.018	-.017
162.4	41094	5.00	4.86	-.14	4.93	1.0144	1.052	4.79	.9580	1.029	-.023	-.022
163.4	41112	5.00	4.80	-.20	4.87	1.0146	1.053	4.67	.9340	1.018	-.035	-.034
164.5	41226	4.98	4.92	-.06	4.76	.9675	1.033	4.70	.9438	1.023	-.010	-.010
165.5	41250	4.97	5.27	.30	4.12	.7818	.947	4.42	.8893	.998	.051	.051
166.5	41327	4.95	5.21	.26	3.98	.7639	.938	4.24	.8566	.984	.046	.047
167.5	41310	4.96	5.13	.17	3.91	.7622	.937	4.08	.8226	.967	.030	.031
168.5	41139	4.98	5.10	.12	3.83	.7510	.932	3.95	.7932	.953	.019	.020
169.5	41361	4.94	5.08	.14	3.75	.7382	.925	3.89	.7874	.950	.025	.026
170.5	41448	4.92	5.05	.13	3.65	.7228	.917	3.78	.7683	.940	.013	.014
171.5	41448	4.92	5.02	.10	3.57	.7112	.911	3.67	.7459	.929	.018	.019
172.5	41565	4.89	5.00	.11	3.47	.6940	.902	3.58	.7321	.922	.020	.022
173.5	41496	4.91	4.98	.07	3.38	.6787	.893	3.45	.7026	.906	.013	.014
174.5	41334	4.93	4.97	.04	3.31	.6660	.886	3.35	.6795	.894	.008	.009
175.5	41550	4.90	4.94	.04	3.27	.6619	.884	3.31	.6755	.892	.008	.009
176.5	41475	4.91	4.92	.01	3.20	.6504	.877	3.21	.6538	.879	.002	.002
177.5	41613	4.88	4.90	.02	3.14	.6406	.872	3.16	.6475	.876	.004	.004
178.5	41646	4.88	4.88	0	3.09	.6332	.867	3.09	.6332	.867	0	0
179.5	41655	4.88	4.86	-.02	3.05	.6276	.864	3.03	.6209	.860	-.004	-.005
180.5	41751	4.85	4.85	0	2.98	.6144	.856	2.98	.6144	.856	0	0
181.5	41674	4.87	4.84	-.03	2.93	.6054	.851	2.90	.5955	.845	-.006	-.007
182.5	41838	4.83	4.82	-.01	2.84	.5832	.841	2.83	.5859	.839	-.002	-.002
183.5	41832	4.83	4.81	-.02	2.76	.5738	.832	2.74	.5673	.827	-.005	-.006
184.5	41913	4.82	4.80	-.02	2.72	.5667	.827	2.70	.5602	.823	-.004	-.005
185.5	41895	4.82	4.78	-.04	2.65	.5544	.819	2.61	.5415	.812	-.007	-.009
186.5	41931	4.82	4.77	-.05	2.57	.5388	.810	2.52	.5228	.799	-.011	-.014
187.5	42100	4.77	4.76	-.01	2.51	.5273	.802	2.50	.5241	.800	-.002	-.002
188.5	42129	4.76	4.70	-.06	2.45	.5213	.798	2.39	.5021	.785	-.013	-.016
189.5	42210	4.75	4.74	-.01	2.40	.5063	.788	2.39	.5032	.786	-.002	-.002

Figure B-12 (f) Flight 9, 14 October 1947, concluded. (NASA Photo EC93 42307-33)

in theory it would do this; for some of us, it was extremely difficult to keep ink from smearing).

The symbol makers were distributed by people in the report editing office. The first set of symbol makers was easy to obtain. Subsequent sets were harder to get. They didn't take names, but they did remember if you asked for more symbol makers very often. Because the symbol makers were flat, they made good page markers; however, their flatness also made them difficult to find in reports or under layers of paper. Some people preferred the clear symbol makers for plotting, but the orange ones were easier to find.

Figures B-15 (b), (c) and (d) show the triangles and curves used in plotting.† The triangles were primarily used as tracing guides when drawing the axis lines and in determining the slope lines for the data. The curves were used as tracing guides for

† The smaller curves were commonly called French curves and the larger ones (over 12 inches) were called ship curves. However, some consider the more intricate curves French curves and the flowing ones, ship curves. Some consider that a curve with a flowing shape, regardless of size, was a ship curve. This last definition is supported by the label in a box of curves that was used by the women computers. The label for the Copenhagen Ship Curves showed flowing curves from 2 to 20 inches in length.

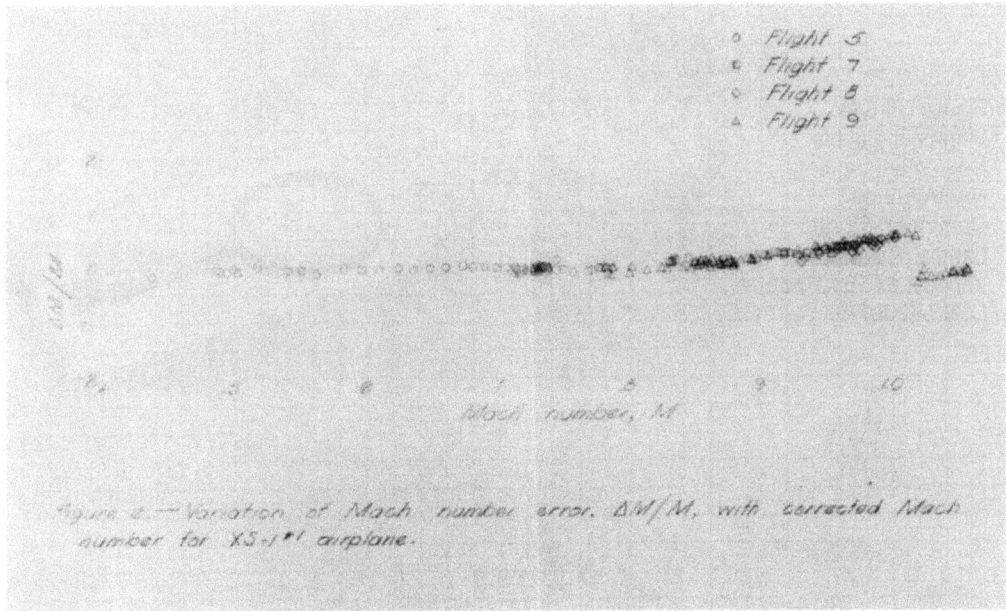

Figure B-13. Mach number position error curve from the XS-1 #1 data; hand plotted by Roxanah Yancey in 1947. (NASA Photo EC93 42307-39)

Figure B-14. Example data sheets, calibration curve and tools used to obtain the final Mach number curve. (NASA Photo EC93 42307-5)

† The ship curves used by the women computers were kept in a box at Roxanah Yancey's desk. When a computer needed a curve, she borrowed and then returned it. The engineers usually borrowed from each other. Some engineers were better at borrowing than returning.

the faired lines that connected the data points. Figure B-16 shows the wide assortment of curves in making the time history plots from an X-15 aircraft flight. The data lines in these plots clearly illustrate that one curve would not be enough to make all the required changes in direction and slope. Because the data for a particular parameter, such as Mach number, would have a similar shape for each flight, certain curves would be better than others for connecting the data points. This fact resulted in people having a

preference for certain curves and putting their names on them. Figure B-17 shows identifying inscriptions on a triangle and a curve. These inscriptions and other markings helped recover the curves in case they were borrowed.† The triangle shown in Figure B-17 is the same one shown in Figure B-15 (b). The triangle was left by Roxanah Yancey when she retired (her name is on the triangle but not visible in the photograph). I know she left it in good condition. Subsequent owners did not treat it as carefully as she did.

59

Figure B-15 (a) Magnifying glass. Note labels on box, NACA Muroc Computer #3, and on handle, Roxanah Yancey. (NASA Photo EC93 42307-9)

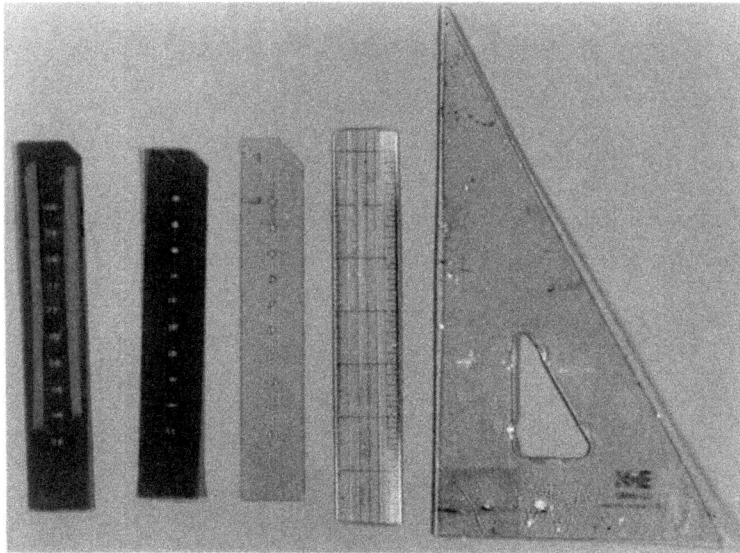

Figure B-15 (b) Left to right: three symbol makers, film scale and triangle. (NASA Photo EC93 42307-10)

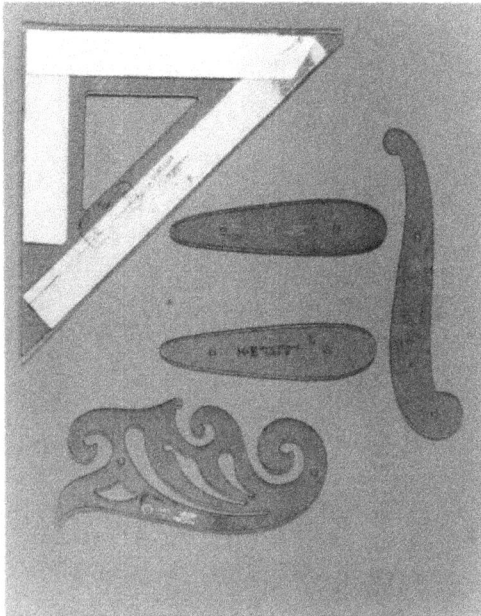

Figure B-15 (c) Small curves (7.25 inches or shorter) and triangle. (NASA Photo EC93 42307-12)

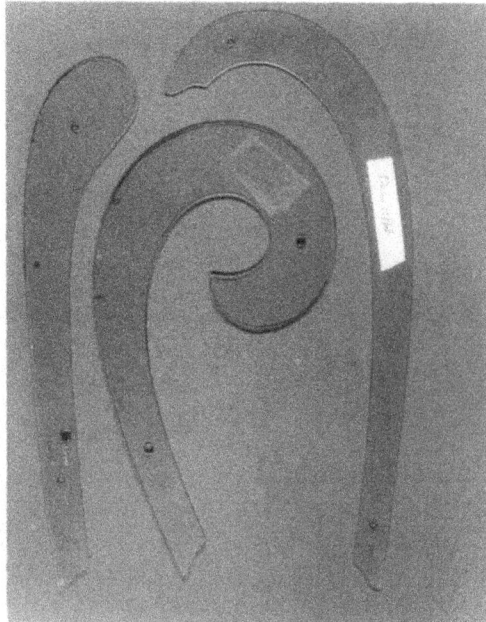

Figure B-15 (d) Large curves (11 inches or longer). (NASA Photo EC93 42307-11)

Figure B-15. Some of the tools used by the computers and engineers.

† This X-15 time history plot, including all the labels external to the plotting area, measures approximately 29 by 29 inches. The original plot used 10 x 10 to the square centimeter paper. This photograph is from an ozalid copy. The Ozalid process used a sensitized paper developed by using a heat process and ammonia. Ozalid copies had dark blue lines and text on a light blue background. The darkness of the lines and the background could be varied in the reproduction process. The ozalid copies could be made with individual sheets in the standard 8 1/2 by 11 and 11 by 17 sizes or could use rolls of paper for larger non-standard sizes such as this copy. Orange carbon-type paper (which only left a coating on the back of the original) was used on the axes, text, curves and data points. The coating could either be applied as the plot was made or the plot could be retraced afterwards. Changes were difficult to make to a plot after the orange coating was applied. The outer layer of the orange coating could be scraped off but you usually had to scrape off some of the paper itself to completely remove the coating. The orange coating required extra effort but significantly improved the contrast for data curves, text, drawings, etc. The ozalid copies were either given to other people to use or were employed as working copies. By using the ozalid copies as working copies, changes to the original figures were minimized. The copy processes used in the 1940s included what looked like a blueprint copy. The curves, data points, gridline and text showed as white on a blue background. The photograph of the calibration curve in figure B-11 was from a 'blueprint' copy. The calibration curve was plotted on paper with 10 by 10 gridlines to the half-inch square. People often had preferences for either the centimeter or half-inch paper. The squares were smaller on the centimeter paper, which provided a larger range for your axis scale than was possible with the half-inch paper.

Figure B-16. X-15 time history plot with curves used for the data lines. Flight log (8.5 by 11 inches) shown for size comparison. (NASA Photo EC93 42307-8)

Figure B-17. Close-up of curve and triangle showing inscriptions. NACA Computer #18 on curve and NACA Muroc computers on triangle.

X-15 Time History and Event Log

Figure B-18 shows the X-15 plot in more detail. This plot is a time history from launch to landing of the velocity, altitude, Mach number, and dynamic pressure.† A plot of these parameters was made for each flight beginning approximately with flight 19 of the program and was the official record for that flight. (There was a total of 199 flights in the program.) Prior to the X-15 program, the X-airplane programs were mainly one-discipline (or at least limited-discipline)

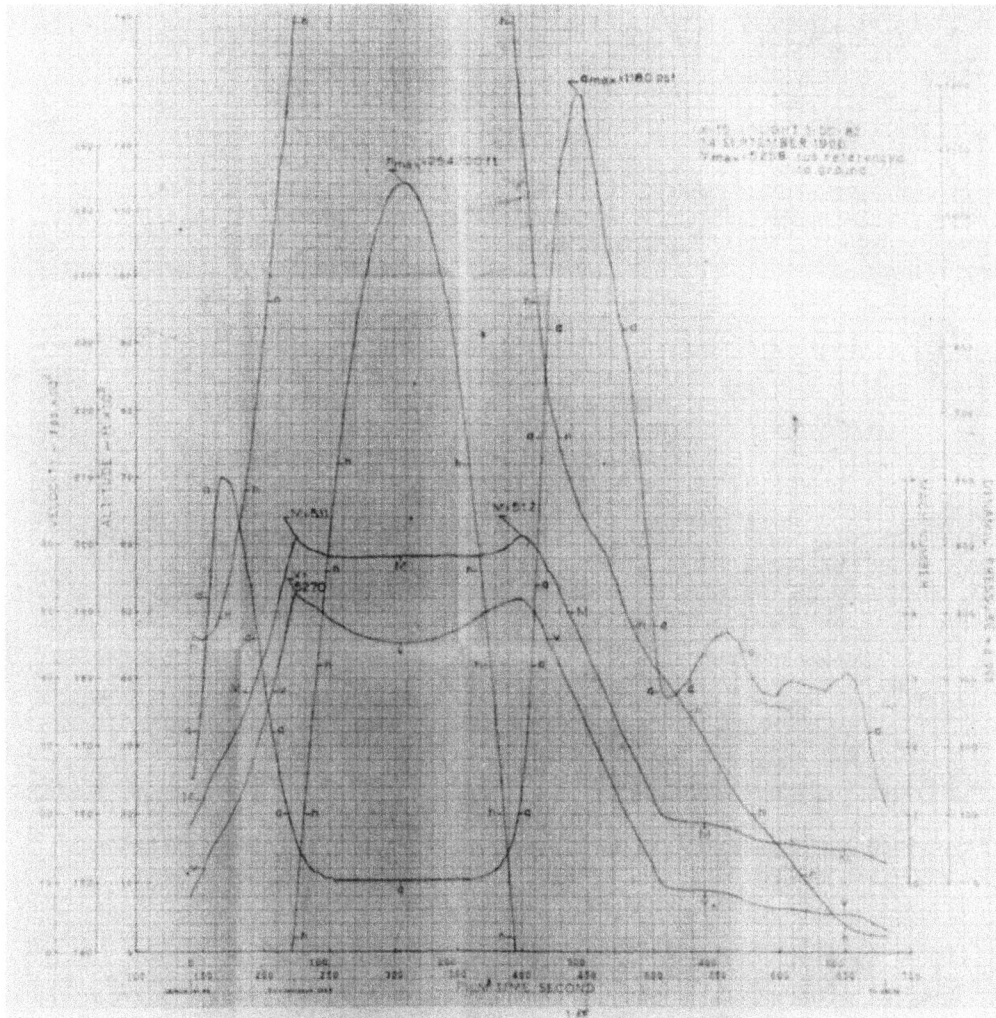

Figure B-18. X-15-3 time history plot of velocity, altitude, Mach number and dynamic pressure from launch to touchdown for flight on 14 September 1966. Note the altitude has a double scale. (NASA Photo EC93 42307-27)

† A discussion of the techniques and instrumentation used to generate the X-15 time history plots is found in: Lannie D. Webb, *Characteristics and use of X-15 Air-Data Sensors* (Washington, D.C.: NASA TN D-4597, 1968)

†† Two B-52 motherships carried the X-15 aloft for launch from under the wing. Figures 19 and 20 show B-52 airplane number 008 and Figure 18 shows the three X-15 aircraft. B-52 number 003 was the other launch aircraft; it was retired at the end of the X-15 program.

studies. The people working in that discipline would do their own version of the X-15 time history plot, at least until the calibrations needed to generate these curves were established. After that, the calculations for obtaining these values were routine enough that the women computers would generate the curves. However, the X-15 changed this. The experiments on the aircraft included many disciplines, and a common, or official, set of values was needed. In addition, obtaining these values was more complex than before. The altitude and Mach number flight envelope for the X-15 ranged from a maximum altitude of 354,200 ft to the altitude at touchdown and for Mach numbers up to 6.70 (4520 mph). This flight envelope required the integration of data from onboard sensors, radiosonde balloons, and radar tracking.† The result was

that an engineering group was formed whose task was to create these plots for each flight.

When Mach number or any of these parameters were needed to analyze data from a flight, the value was read from the time-history plot for the desired time. For example, for a film time of 300 seconds, Mach number, altitude, velocity, and dynamic pressure are 4.82, 253,000 feet (ft), 4540 feet per second (fps) and 3 pounds per square foot (psf), respectively. Corresponding values at 400 seconds are 5.12, 126,000 ft, 5198 fps, and 130 psf. As can seen in Figure B-18, the time scale shows two different times. One is the film time which starts at 100 seconds. The zero film time (not shown) is when the film recorders were started. The second time scale shows the time in seconds from launch.†† The

† Scale from 0 to 6000 fps.

†† Scale from 0 to 6.

††† Scale from 0 to 1200 psf.

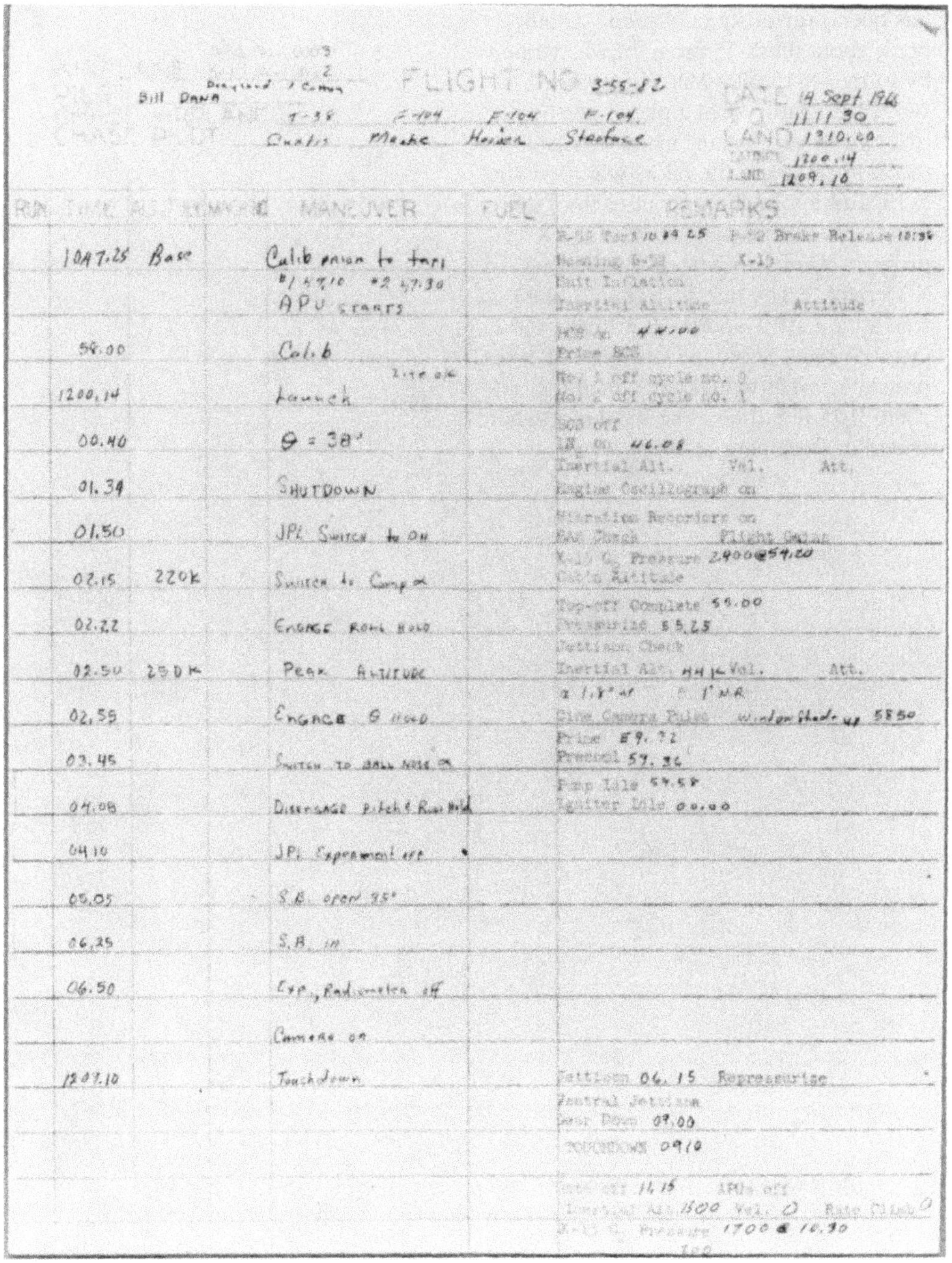

Figure B-19. Event log for X-15-3 flight on 14 September 1966. (NASA Photo EC9342307-36)

scales for velocity (the data curve marked "v")† and altitude (the data curve marked "h") are on the left side. Note that altitude has a double scale, 0 to 140,000 ft and 140,000 ft to 260,000 ft. The altitude is the height above sea level, which is why the touchdown altitude is 2275 ft, the height above sea level of the dry lakebed runway at Edwards. The scales for Mach number (the data curve marked "M")†† and dynamic pressure (the data curve marked "q")††† are on the right side.

Figure B-19 shows the event log for this flight. Not surprisingly, the sheet is somewhat cryptic to someone not familiar with the X-15 program. For instance, the time 1047.25 is usually written 10:47.25. Some of the abbreviations are: APU - Auxiliary Power Unit; JPL - Jet Propulsion Laboratory; S.B. - Speed Brake; BCS - Ballistic Control System; and SAS - Stability Augmentation System. A good discussion of the development of the X-15 aircraft and the first 5 years of the flight program has been previously published.[†] Another book about the X-15 program was written by former X-15 pilot Milt Thompson.[††] Written primarily from a pilot's perspective, this book contains many details about the X-15 program, the pilots who flew the X-15, and information about each of the flights. Two other papers about the X-15 program were also written by a former X-15 pilot.[†††] The first X-15 (glide) flight was 8 June 1959, and the last flight was 24 October 1968. Snow in December of 1968 prevented what would have been the 200th X-15 flight. Funding for the program ended in December of 1968.

[†] Wendell H. Stillwell, *X-15 Research Results with a Selected Bibliography* (Washington, D.C.: NASA SP-60, 1965).

[††] Milton O. Thompson, *At the Edge of Space: The X-15 Flight Program* (Washington, D.C.: Smithsonian Institution Press, 1992).

[†††] William H. Dana, "A History of the X-15 Program," Thirty-First Symposium Proceedings of the Society of Experimental Test Pilots, September 23-26, 1987, and "The X-15 Airplane—Lessons Learned" (Washington, D.C.: AIAA-93-0309, 1993).

Appendix C: Women† in the Engineering Field

Women Who Worked as Computers (1946-1954)

Name	Period
Phyllis Rogers Actis	Sometime before October 1947 to early 1950s
Ilene Alexander	1948 to mid-1949
Katharine H. Armistead	1950; 1952 to retirement in 1979 (at Langley between 1950 and 1952); co-author on 1 report in 1957, 1 in 1958, and lead author in 1973
Lilly Ann Bajus	Probably late 1940s to early 1950s
Rozalia M. Bandish	Probably late 1940s early 1950s; co-author on report in 1951
Beverly Jane Swanson Cothren	Probably late 1940s to early 1950s; co-author as Swanson on report in 1950
Joan M. Childs Dahlen	Probably late 1940s to early 1950s, sole author as Childs on report in 1953
Angel H. Dunn	Probably late 1940s to early 1950s, co-author on report in 1952
Helen N. Foley	1950 to 1960 (Began as women computer but in 1952 established library and editorial office and served as head of that office.)
Mary (Tut) W. Hedgepeth	November 1948 to 1953
Dorothy C. Clift Hughes	Sometime before October 1947 to probably mid 1949; co-author as Clift on 2 reports in 1948
Mary V. Little (married Albert E. Kuhl after retiring)	1949 to retirement in 1973, co-author on report in 1958
Betty J. Scott Love	1952 to retirement in 1973, co-author as Scott on a report in 1957, 1961 and 1963; co-author as Love in 1967 and 1971
Isabell K. Martin	December 1946; left by April 1947
Geraldine C. Mayer	Probably late 1940s to early 1950s; co-author on report in 1950
Mary M. Payne	1948 to early 1951; co-author on report in 1950
Mary Pierce	Probably late 1940s to early 1950s; co-author on report in 1950
Marion Pittman	Probably early 1950s
Dorothy Crawford Roth	April 1947 to early 1949
Lucille E. Sanford	October 1953 to retirement in June 1973
Johnnye (J.) C. Green Sisk	1950 or 1951 to 1955; 1956 to 1959
Emily Stephens	Probably late 1940s to mid 1949
Beverly Smith	Probably late 1940s to early 1950s

J. Delores Sutphin	Around 1954
Peggy L. Sutphin (sister to Delores)	Around 1954
Gertrude (Trudy) V. Wilken Valentine	Probably late 1940s to early 1950s; co-author as Wilken on report in 1950
Helen L. Wall	Probably late 1940s to early 1950s; co-author on report in 1949
Julia B. Woodbridge	Probably late 1940s to early 1950s; co-author on report in 1950
Roxanah B. Yancey	December 1946 to retirement end of June 1973; co-author on 5 reports in 1949, 1971, 1972, 1973 and 1974; lead author in 1962 and 1973, sole author in 1964

Women from 1960 to December 1995
(December 1995 indicated as present under Period)

Bianca Trujillo Anderson	1979[†] to March 1995 (quit)
Katharine H. Armistead	1950; 1952 to retirement in 1979 (also see 1946 to 1954 listing)
Anne Baldwin	Early 1960s; probably from 1960 to 1962 (quit)
Jennifer L. Baer-Riedhart	1974 to present
Catherine Bahm	1993[†] to present (co-op; graduated 1995)
Lisa Jennett Bjarke	1979[†] to present
Carolyn E. Body	End of July 1974 to mid July 1976 (died in glider accident)
Georgina Rodriguez Branco	1986 to present
Marta R. Bohn-Meyer	1979 to present
Dorothea Cohen	1988 to present
Doris A. Myers Dowden	1973 to 1980; 1989 to present
Darla D. Duke	1983 to medical retirement in 1987
Martha B. Evans	1975 to retirement in March 1995
Kimberly A. Ennix	1991 to present
Constance Eaton Harney	1965 to retirement in May 1994
Mary F. Shafer Iliff	1974 to present
Michele Leong Jarvis	Fall 1994 to present (co-op 1990 and 1991)
Beverly Strickland Klein	1961 to end of 1973 (quit)
Donna L. Knighton	1989 to present
Heather H. Lambert	1983 to 1991 (transferred to NASA Lewis)

[†] These women were in the co-op program and returned to Dryden after graduation from college. The year given is when they started in the co-op program with Dryden; the year of graduation could be up to four years later. Women co-ops who were authors but did not return to Dryden after graduation were Diane DeMarco (at Dryden in the early to mid-1970s), Sandra Thornberry Steers (at Dryden in the early to mid-1970s), and Maureen O'Connor (at Dryden in the early 1980s).

Georgene Miltonberger Laub	Mid 1960s, probably 1965 to early 1967 (transferred to NASA Ames)
Jeanette H. Le	1989 to present
Mary V. Little	1949 to retirement in 1973 (also see 1946 to 1954 listing)
Betty J. Scott Love	1952 to retirement in 1973 (also see 1946 to 1954 listing)
Karen S. Green Mackall	1973† to present
Trindel A. Maine	1982 to present
Laurie Marshall	1993 to present
Elsie B. Mc Gowan	1964 to retirement in March 1995
Darlene S. Mosser-Kerner	1989 to present
Cynthia Norman	Fall 1994 to present
Sheryll Goecke Powers	1963† to present
Cynthia M. Privoznik	1981 to 1984 (transferred to Naval Weapons Center, China Lake, California)
Susan Jane Rashkin	1989 to 1991 (quit)
Victoria A. Regenie	1983 to present
Carol A. Bauer Reukauf	1971† to present
Dianne Roux	1966 to 1967 (quit)
Bertha M. Ryan	1960 to late 1966 or early 1967 (transferred to Naval Weapons Center, China Lake, California)
Patricia C. Seamount	1992 to March 1995 (quit)
Karla Shy	Late summer 1994 to present
Harriet J. DeVries Stephenson Smith	1952† to 1983 when she left to work as a congressional aide
Carol S. Tanner	Mid 1960s, probably 1964, to 1966
Lura E. Kern Vernon	1989 to August 1994 (quit)
Roxanah B. Yancey	1946 to retirement in 1973 (also see 1946 to 1954 listing)
Fanny A. Zuniga	1989 to July 1994 (transferred to NASA Ames)

Appendix D: Number of Women by Job Category from 1960 to December 1995

Engineering Disciplines	Computer Programming	Airplane Simulation	Management
1960 - 1969, Total number of women = 14			
10 (includes 3 former woman computers)	3	0	1 chief of Programming and Data Processing Branch (former woman computer)
1970 - 1979, Total number of women = 17			
10 (2 former woman computers retired 1973 and 1 in 1979)	4	1	1 chief of Programming and Data Processing Branch (Retired 1973, former woman computer); 1 in program management
1980 - 1989, Total number of women = 26			
15 (2 instrumentation engineers responsible for research instrumentation on airplane; 1 an operations engineer responsible for flight readiness of airplane)	0	4	3 in program management; 1 chief of branch responsible for computer systems, flight control rooms, and information networks; 3 in non-disciplinary management positions
1990 - 1993, Total number of women = 26			
14 (1 an instrumentation engineer)	0	4	4 in program management (1 an acting deputy chief for program management division; 1 also serves as a flight test engineer on the SR-71 crew);1 deputy chief of division responsible for computer systems, flight control rooms, and information networks (former branch chief); 3 nondisciplinary management

March 1994, Total number of women = 24

13 (1 an instrumentation engineer)	0	3	4 in program management (1 an acting deputy chief for program management division; 1 also serves as a flight test engineer on the SR-71 crew); 1 deputy chief of division responsible for computer systems, flight control rooms, and information networks (former branch chief); 3 nondisciplinary management

December 1995, Total number of women = 21

11 (2 are instrumentation engineers)	0	1	3 in program management (1 also serves as a flight test engineer on the SR-71 crew); 6 nondisciplinary management

Notes: Co-ops not included in numbers. Numbers are maximum for time periods from 1960-1969, 1970-1979, 1980-1989, and 1990-1993.

"Engineering discipline" refers to any of the airplane discipline studies, for example, propulsion, aerodynamics, stability and control, structures, etc.

"Program management" refers to general oversight of an airplane program such as coordinating, scheduling, funding, working with any outside partners involved with the program, etc.

"Nondisciplinary management" includes non-supervisory staff positions and positions that function primarily as a focal point to coordinate requests between engineering groups.

Index

List of Figures

List of Tables

About the Author

Sheryll Goecke Powers began working at the NASA Flight Research Center at the end of May 1963 in a NASA-university work-study program for students. After graduation, she returned to the Center, renamed in honor of Hugh L. Dryden in 1976, as an aerospace engineer and worked in the area of airplane drag and local flow studies. The labor-intensive data reduction techniques she used in the 1960s were the same as those used for the first X-plane programs. These techniques were at first altered and then replaced by techniques that used the immense calculating and processing capabilities of the digital computer. During her career, she has written and served as co-author on several NASA technical reports. Her two non-technical reports are "A Brief History of Women in the Engineering Field at Dryden from 1946 to November 1992" (Proceedings, the Society of Women Engineers 1993 National Convention and Student Conference, Chicago, Illinois, June 21-27, 1993) and "A Biased Historical Perspective of Women in the Engineering Field at Dryden from 1946 to November 1992" (NASA CP-10134, 1994), which are both shorter versions of this study. Ms. Powers earned a BS in aerospace engineering from Iowa State University in 1967 and an MS and Eng. Deg., also in aerospace engineering, from the University of Southern California in 1971 and 1976 respectively.

Monographs in Aerospace History

This is the sixth publication in a series of special studies prepared under the auspices of the NASA History Program. The Monographs in Aerospace History series is designed to provide a wide variety of investigations relative to the history of aeronautics and space. These publications are intended to be tightly focused in terms of subject, relatively short in length, and reproduced in inexpensive format to allow timely and broad dissemination to researchers in aerospace history. Suggestions for additional publications in the Monographs in Aerospace History series are welcome and should be sent to Roger D. Launius, Chief Historian, Code ZH, National Aeronautics and Space Administration, Washington, DC, 20546. Previous publications in this series are:

Launius, Roger D. and Gillette, Aaron K. Compilers. *Toward a History of the Space Shuttle: An Annotated Bibliography.* (Number 1, 1992)

Launius, Roger D. and Hunley, J. D. Compilers. *An Annotated Bibliography of the Apollo Program.* (Number 2, 1994)

Launius, Roger D. *Apollo: A Retrospective Analysis.* (Number 3, 1994)

Hansen, James R. *Enchanted Rendezvous: John C. Houbolt and the Genesis of the Lunar-Orbit Rendezvous Concept.* (Number 4, 1995)

Gorn, Michael H. *Hugh L. Dryden's Career in Aviation and Space.* (Number 5, 1996)